CW00434304

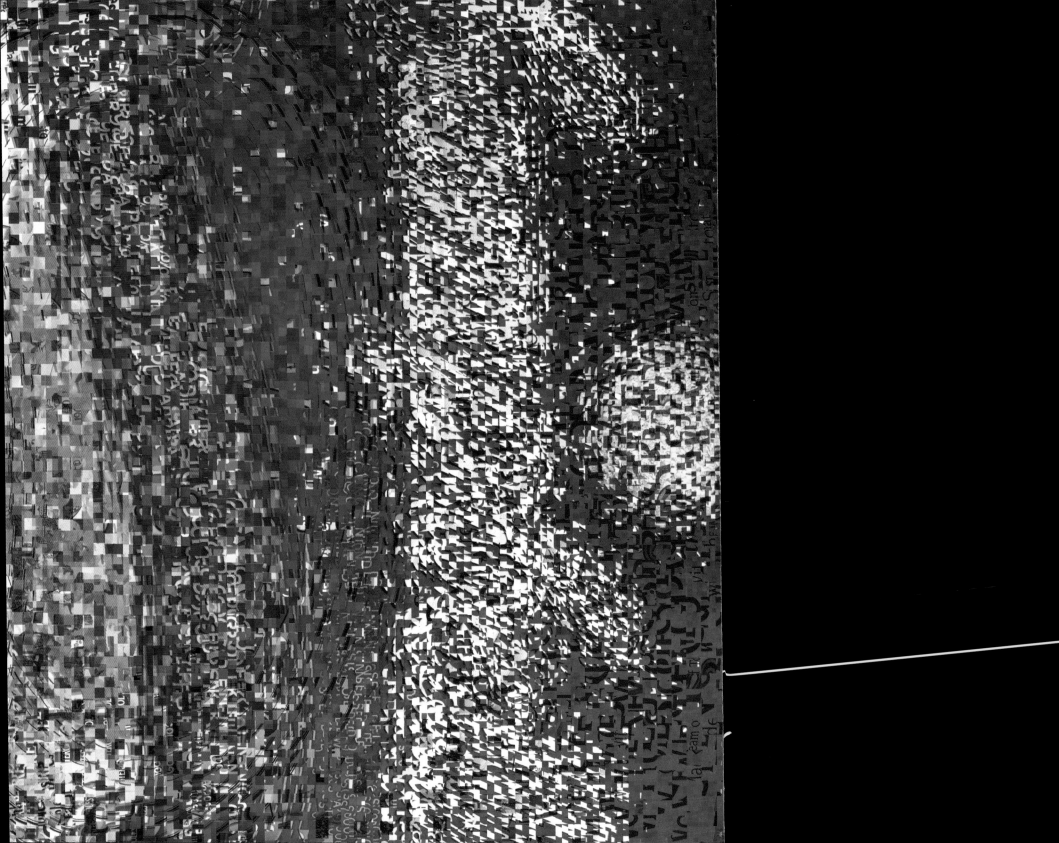

Creative Code

With over 600 illustrations

John Maeda

Foreword by Red Burns

First published in the United Kingdom in 2004 by Thames & Hudson Ltd, 181A High Holborn, London WC1V 7QX

www.thamesandhudson.com

© 2004 John Maeda

British Library Cataloguing-in-Publication Data
A catalogue record for this book is available from the British Library

ISBN 0-500-28517-9

Printed and bound in China by Midas Printing

Designed by John Maeda

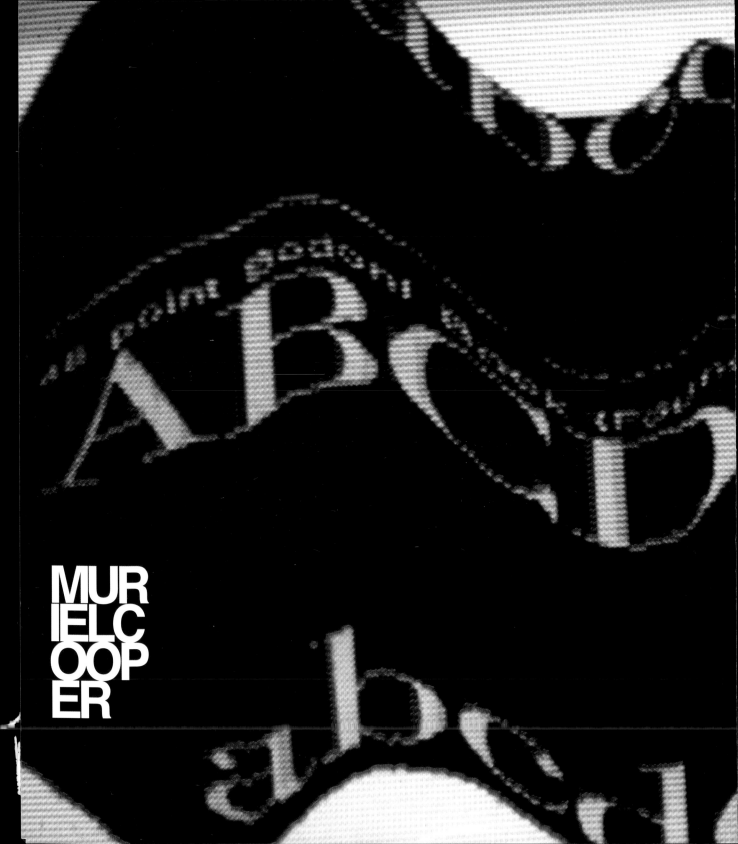

MUR
IELC
OOP
ER

*"I was convinced that the line
between reproduction tools
and design would blur when
information became electronic
and that the lines between designer
and artist, author and designer,
professional and amateur would
also dissolve."*

**In memory of
Muriel Cooper, 1925–94**

as per thought it
i) the beginning
why must we paint ...?

people today... security is code.
it is like being chained (to) symbols

① establish a
② (video)
③

website is the modern day
equivalent of the great
cathedral.

They ... do not
... future,
... the future

Table of contents

Foreword: Interview with Red Burns

I decided to depart from the normal format of a foreword as I have always felt that the main reason for this section is to have the rare opportunity to get to know someone who can see the real "big picture." Red Burns was the only person I had in mind because I find Red so inspiring that I want to share her unusual breed of thinking with you. So, I conducted a mini interview with her when we were both in Philadelphia for a conference in 2003.

Where were you born?
Ottawa, Canada.

What is your family background?
My parents were immigrants. They believed that school was where it all had to happen. I happened to like school. But, I was stuck in a system where I skipped three grades, which was socially horrible. I literally had no friends. I was eleven and everyone else was fourteen. I was smaller, skinnier, paler, and freckle-faced ... so I lived in books. Books were my salvation.

I graduated from high school at the age of sixteen. My mother said that I couldn't stay at home. "What am I going to do?" I asked. She said, "You'll be able to figure it out, but you just can't stay at home." I wasn't married and I couldn't get a job.

I loved reading so much that I spent every day at the library. When I turned seventeen, I bumped into a fellow I had gone to school with. He said, "I'm having a party on Saturday night." I felt awkward and gawky at the time and remember asking my mom, "What shall I do?" She said nothing would ever happen if I just stayed at home.

My life changed at that party. I was standing in the corner and my eyes fell on the most incredible looking person I had ever seen (at that time) across the room. I was so connected to this fellow and I stared so hard that the guy came over. He asked me my name, and I said, "Toni." He then said, "Do you ride horses?" I replied, "Of course." I'd never been on a horse. "Give me your telephone number and I'll take you riding," he said.

He came to my house the next week in a taxi. A taxi! Imagine that! Being the child of an immigrant, I was brought up to believe that you never used a taxi unless there was a life-threatening emergency. Anyway, I got on the horse, and I didn't care if it killed me. We went riding, and I was thrown several times.

One day we hung out near the Canadian National Film Board, and the next day I decided to get a job there. I had no qualifications, so I sat outside John Grierson's door every day for three weeks. Each day I asked for a job, and he flatly replied, "No." I refused to take no for an answer.

One day he relented, saying, "Go to this address on Monday." I went; there was a sign that said "National Film Board Distribution," and inside there were desks and typewriters but no film. Just papers. I thought, "There's been a mistake!"

I remember the first person I met there—Tom Buchanan. He said, "What is it with you? You have no talent. You're not an animator, or an editor, or a negative cutter, or a sound man, or a camera man." I told him, "I want to learn," and he said, "We have no time for learning."

So, I went back to Grierson and he said, "One more chance," sending me to work for Raymond Spottiswoode who was writing a book called *A Grammar of the Film*, which happens to be one of the seminal books on film. Because I was so familiar with libraries, the author gave me chapters to proofread. Although I knew nothing about film, I knew more than enough about books. We developed a relationship in which I'd read the book and tell him what I didn't understand and he'd say, "Oh, you're stupid!" I'd retort, "No, no, no. I'm not stupid—I can read." Meanwhile, his real job was to organize the system for making films, which nobody knew how to do in 1942; instead, people went here to get a camera, there to get recording equipment, and so on. But, he never did this because he was writing his book. I did it instead. That's how I learned to make a film. I figured out the whole system. I then began to find my way with people who were a good ten years older than me and came from exotic places, while I was this extremely provincial skinny kid. That was the beginning of my interest in visual communication.

What were your favorite books as a child?
Libraries in those years were run by librarians. I went through all the Russian and French writers. My favorite book, and I realize now I understood nothing because I thought I understood everything, was Leo Tolstoy's *War and Peace*. I loved that book but all I really cared about was the romance with Natasha. I also loved the *Brothers Karamazov* by Fyodor Dostoevsky and *Magic Mountain* by Thomas Mann. I never thought these books were about real people or places; I thought they had nothing to do with real life. Nothing. Then, when I got to the film board, I was in this group of amazing people, and I became the mascot because I was the kid.

Did you have good teachers in life?
Incredible teachers. I knew then that they were special, but I didn't have anything to

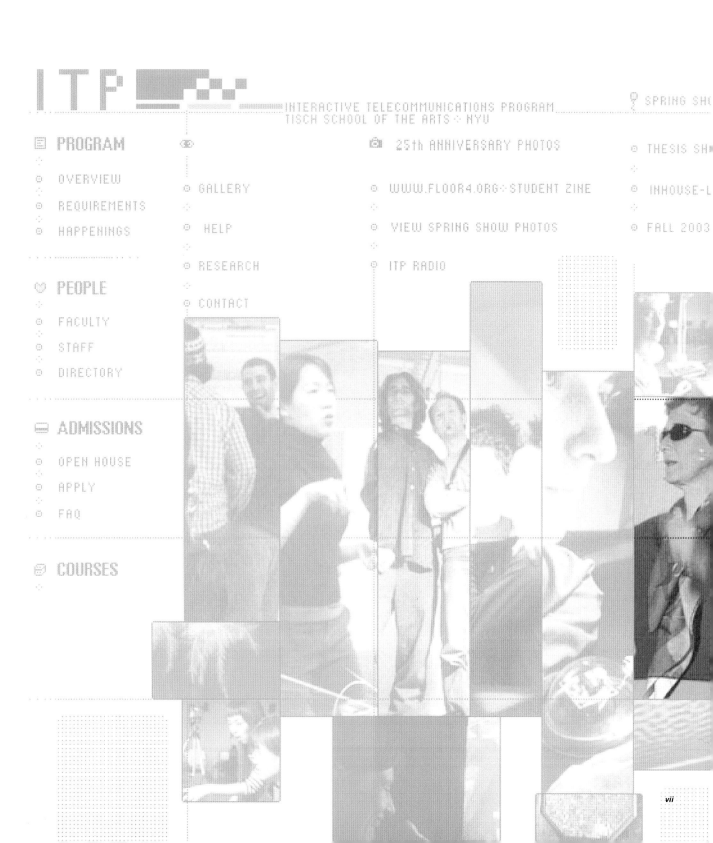

ITP

▤ PROGRAM

◉ 25th ANNIVERSARY PHOTOS

◎ THESIS SH⬦

◎ OVERVIEW

◎ GALLERY

◎ WWW.FLOOR4.ORG ⬦ STUDENT ZINE

◎ INHOUSE-L

◎ REQUIREMENTS

◎ HAPPENINGS

◎ HELP

◎ VIEW SPRING SHOW PHOTOS

◎ FALL 2003

◎ RESEARCH

◎ ITP RADIO

♡ PEOPLE

◎ CONTACT

◎ FACULTY

◎ STAFF

◎ DIRECTORY

▭ ADMISSIONS

◎ OPEN HOUSE

◎ APPLY

◎ FAQ

▣ COURSES

compare them against. At the time, I didn't understand why so many people hated work. I had no idea. I thought the concept of communication with pictures was a startling one.

Where did your experiences lead you?

When I was twenty-two, I had my first kid (of three) and decided to be a full-time mother. I didn't go back to work for about seven years.

When I finally did, it was in the then new field of television. It had just been introduced to Canada—that was in the mid-1950s. My first husband died when I was twenty-eight, and when I was thirty-four or thirty-five I married again. I had another kid and we moved to New York. My husband's job was with Columbia Pictures and we traveled around quite a bit, so much so that I couldn't work due to all our movement. I spent eleven unbelievable years traveling all over the world. It was like, "Hello!" I was no longer this provincial girl.

In 1970, somebody showed me a film recorder camera, and I had an epiphany! My god, people can make their own documents. What did that mean? I taught a class about video at New York University (NYU) and a strange thing happened. Someone from the Markle Foundation handed me his card when I was explaining that people can take control of their lives, can make their own documents, and shouldn't feel beholden to anyone. You see, there were only three networks then: ABC, NBC, and CBS and if you weren't with one of them, you had no say. This guy was fired up and said I should write a piece. "You'd fund something?" I asked. "Maybe," he replied. I wrote up a proposal, and he acknowledged it was interesting but added, "Where's the budget?" Budget? I knew how to produce a film budget but not this kind of budget.

"Will you help me?" I asked. He did. I received $260,000 from the Markle Foundation to set up the Alternate Media Center (AMC) at NYU in 1970. I had no idea how to do it, so when the money came in, I called the dean. He was hesitant,

"You can't do that—raise money without permission." I replied, "Well, it's here. If you don't want it you can send it back." A relationship evolved in which I was completely autonomous, and that was the start of the AMC.

The AMC had me working with people, cameras, and communication. We answered a request from the National Science Foundation about delivering social services on two-way television. We had to study whether the costs were beneficial; I knew nothing about this, but I was at a university with people from so many disciplines. So we created a little group consisting of a gerontologist, a political scientist, an economist, and a sociologist to work out how to set up access centers all around the USA. We got $1.75 million to set up this thing that I knew nothing about nor whether it was cost effective. We were paid $100,000 to write a proposal and, after initial approval, we formed our first local research group at Redding. One thing we clearly could not do without was input from the people who lived there. I ended up getting to know all the people there, even the mayor.

To create the two-way TV, we overlaid it on the old cable system, reversed the amplifiers and had signals going out to the head-ends. In effect, we had designed an economical means of doing two-way TV without adding new cables to the system. That's where the idea came from to offer a graduate program on which people worked with such new technologies as small cameras and cable television. Individuals could do their own production and distribution, cutting out the middleman (the networks). It was like a closed book.

Did computers change the ITP?

Not at all. That's a really important point: It has never been about the tools. It has always been about people—how people use technology, and how these technologies can help people communicate.

We don't have the answers. We are still looking, trying, challenging you to figure it

out. When computing began, I called up a friend at Atari and said, "I'd like a dozen." He responded, "We have a foundation and you have to apply." I said, "No way!" As a result, we got a dozen computers. At the ITP, which focuses on cable technologies, the addition of the computer was nothing special, it was just another crayon in the box next to video or sound.

What is the key to learning?

I value people's imagination—their sense of freedom to express—because I think everyone has imagination. I don't think imagination is ever thought of as practical. My job was to create an environment that encouraged people to fail. By encouraging them to fail, they would then try something they would not usually do as there were no penalties. I never directed, I never said it had to be like this or like that. Nothing complicated, it was not a big deal.

Inspiration is hard. You can't define it. You can only have it. My aim has always been to encourage people and to get them started doing things they never thought they could. To me life is a wonderment. A total fucking wonderment. I have never thought I knew, because I'm always discovering. To spend my time with people that are talented and young is the greatest gift.

People have to learn how to learn. What was it that Gregory Bateson said? "Information is a difference that makes a difference." I always ask myself, "What is the difference that makes the difference, that takes it out of the ordinary?"

I have never been afraid. Fear and lack of confidence are inhibiting factors. I have always tried to extract these two afflictions from my students because fear paralyzes.

Preface

I see display screens everywhere, and I wonder whether they are happy. Happy? Well, maybe "happy" is not the right word. Instead, "Do they live meaningful lives?" may be the question to ask.

As I continue to age and learn more about this world, I find it more apt to ask this question of the people around me rather than the displays. After all, in this digital age, computers seem to get considerably more attention than people.

How much do we need to know about the computer to survive? I once held strongly that to know the art of programming—or "coding," which is the trendier term—is the critical skill for any developing digital artist or designer. Today, I no longer feel this way. I think it is useful for people to appreciate the underlying technologies that drive digital expression, however, that knowledge alone is not a primary factor in achieving excellence or advancement in the medium.

→
Computers appear to be winning the battle between human and computer. We all have to work a little harder!

2001

human 26,700,000
computer 42,300,000

2002

human 38,100,000
computer 53,900,000

If there were a prerequisite for the future successful digital creative, it would be the passion for discovery—something that has been around a lot longer than the computer. How is this desire instilled in us? By the few people we meet in our life who give us courage; people like Red Burns and Muriel Cooper.

A student at Carnegie Mellon University asked me, "Are all the visionaries gone? I can't find one anywhere." My response was that the fact she seeks them at all is evidence that someday she will find them, and maybe even the visionary that lies within herself. From the kind of determination and energy she displayed, I am certain she is well on her way.

There is one secret well of passion known to all educators. It derives not from their own masters, but from the students with whose futures they are entrusted. There is an unlimited passion for discovery among the young, which can lead to outcomes that are misguided and should remain unspoken but that are more often spot on. This book is a collection of discoveries borne of naivety and bravery that I witnessed whilst working with some extraordinarily talented students from such diverse backgrounds as astrophysics, mathematics, graphic design and the fine arts. I hope that you will share in their unwitting gifts of clarity, and give true meaning to their hard work by sitting back and enjoying the show.

John Maeda, 2004
Lexington, Massachusetts

2003

human 133,000,000

computer 205,000,000

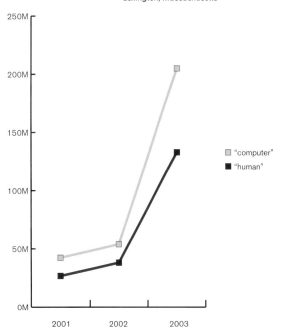

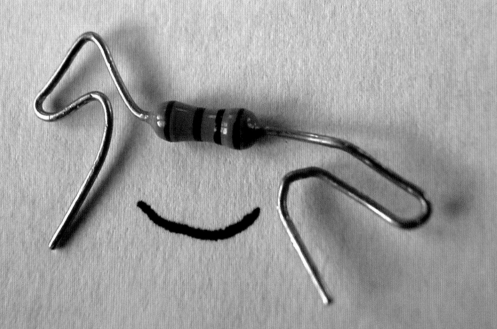

1. Resume

I made the book *MAEDA@MEDIA* to close out a period of thought and practice that I believed had reached its artistic and philosophical fruition, and to create a time capsule of another person (my old self). As I saw a new generation rapidly approaching, it seemed more dignified to hang up my mouse and get out of the way rather than to engage in brutal mouse-to-mouse combat with someone with more vitality than myself. I went to the physical edges of my human existence to create the book, and although there are perhaps many things I wish I had done differently, as a documentation, manifesto, and monograph, it serves its purpose fine.

Since *MAEDA@MEDIA,* an increasing number of visitors have come to my office at the MIT Media Lab in an attempt to debunk my ideas. Somehow, they would try to prove to me and the rest of the world that I was like other high-tech digital gurus who knew little about the inner-workings of computers, and much less about how to operate the beasts. After being subject to many forced exorcisms I began to change (as I note in my preface to this book); I do not care as much about programming as I used to. Perspective counts for at least fifty percent (and growing).

Sure, I can hack codes with the geekiest of thoroughbred programmers, and operate all these programs for desktop publishing that drive me crazy every day. I have the advanced RSI to prove it. I wish I had learned to play the piano when I was younger to understand better keyboard posture, because pianists (and hunt-and-peck typists) seem to go on strong even with age. Touch-typing was my hobby as a youth, which in retrospect was great for programming but terrible for making friends.

I have always given one mandate to my students: "Don't think, just do." I would like to think that was my original maxim, but Google.com tells me that the poet Horace (65–8 B.C.) had already figured it out. I am happy to report, however, that, in spite of growing responsibilities, I continue to just do.

LIGHT BOXES
Cristinerose Gallery, 2000

Shortly after the publication of *MAEDA@MEDIA,* I was drafted into an administrative position at the Media Lab. I learned a great deal from this move, perhaps the most important thing was to acknowledge what you can do, and what you cannot do at a given time in your life. Previously, I had thought it was forbidden to think you cannot do something. On the contrary, it is better to recognize your limits to best assess the obstacles that sit before you and in so doing to prepare the engine that will propel you past the challenge.

During this period as a form of meditation I created a series of six boxes, called "Light Boxes," constructed from MDF and handcrafted computer circuitry. Inside each box is a different configuration of green LEDs, which are lit at varying intervals. The boxes function as puzzles or are based around a theme, such as communication, and are operated by foot with a single hand-milled aluminium button.

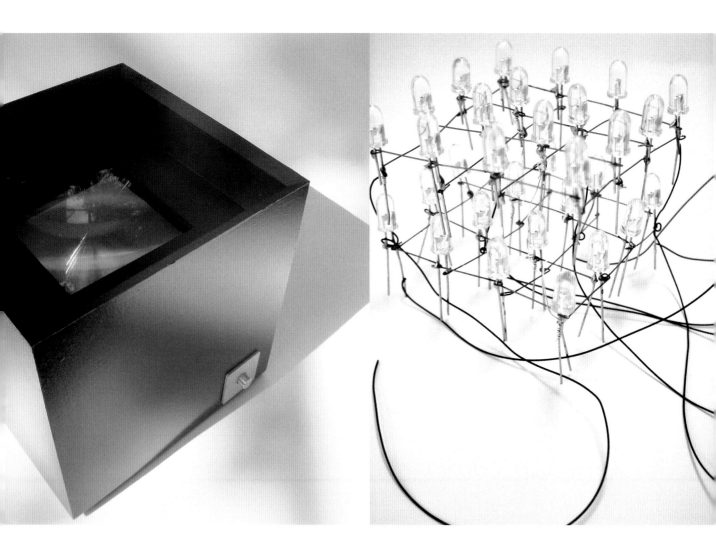

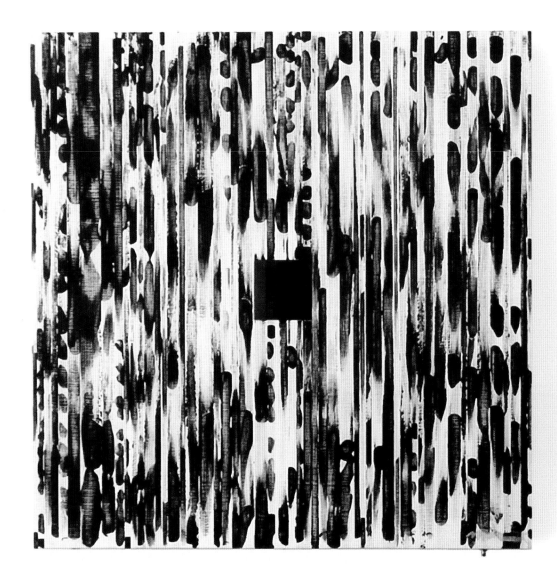

I have never liked the idea of art supply stores because the implication is that art cannot be made unless you shop there first. So, I went to the local Home Depot (a home improvement chain) to gather some materials and to Staples (an office supply chain) to pick up ten Palm hand-held computers. I constructed a series of flat boxes, which I painted in a mix of abstract styles. I embedded a Palm computer in each of the paintings (the small black square above) and specifically programmed each one to visually "think" about what the painting signified. The Palm Paintings, as they are called, are my attempt to create a mirroring of virtual and physical abstractions, where one abstraction informs the other.

PALM PAINTINGS
Cristinerose Gallery, 2000

PROCESS BLOCKS
Cristinerose Gallery, 2000

Around the same time as I worked on the Palm Paintings, I purchased some roughly cut, scrap plastic blocks. After spending four months in the MIT workshop milling the surfaces smooth by machine and by hand, I violated each surface with such stimuli as a hammer, fire, and an ink-jet printer. Each act of degradation was recorded dynamically as a lenticular imprint on the main face of each block. My aim was to experience the blocks from their re-birth as an innocent, perfect form all the way through to their return to imperfection.

The blue masking tape I used to protect the pristine faces of each block became a passion in itself for me. I used so much that it began to possess me to coat everything in blue tape.

CODED BLUE
California College of the Arts/Logan Galleries, 2000

For a one-man show under curator Marina McDougall, I created an installation using blue masking tape, which continued my theme of mirrored abstractions. A laptop taped to the window provided the virtual counter-representation of the physical space.

Spread across the seven galleries of the NTT ICC in Tokyo, my mid-career retrospective was curated by Shoji Itoh, with exhibition design by Naoto Fukasawa. One hundred prints, seventy projectors, and eighty desktop computers defined the space of this massive exhibition. An unbroken, 100-meter-long print-out from the Dai Nippon Printing One Line Project was the unifying element that hung the length of the gallery spaces. The main hall was an impressive spectacle, with such input devices as keyboards, mice, and trackballs extruded in perfection on columns that rose seamlessly from the floor.

The inspiration behind "CD Crash" was the exaggerated action with which the early PowerMac G3 ejected CDs. I felt it was so dangerous that it needed to be

properly examined, the way that cars are tested for safety. The Color Classic signaled with a series of beeps to the G3 that it was ready, and the G3 ejected the CD

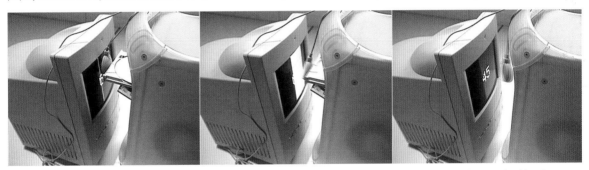

into the Color Classic's microphone. The sound energy was accumulated and a numerical score displayed. Surprisingly, this ran for three months without issues.

JOHN MAEDA: POST DIGITAL
NTT InterCommunication Center, 2001

Housed in one of the smaller galleries was my collection of old computers. I reinterpreted each of them as interactive installations to give them new life.

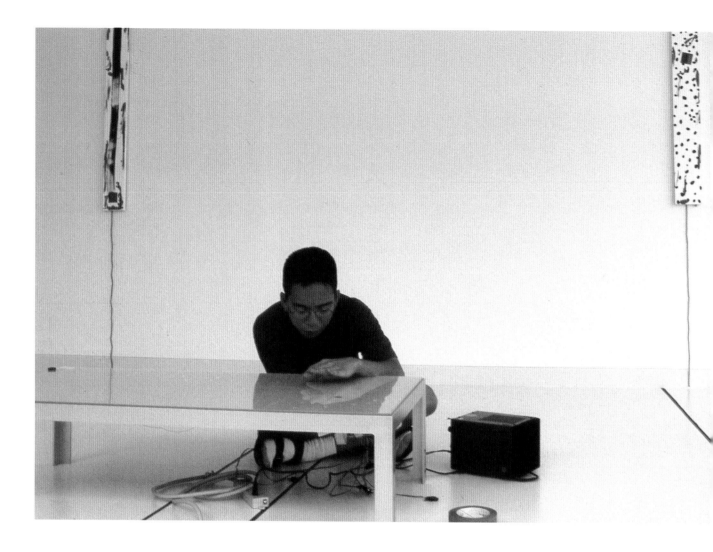

JOHN MAEDA: POST DIGITAL
NTT InterCommunication Center, 2001

In the smallest gallery of the ICC was an experiment in furniture design I had begun with Sawaya & Moroni of Italy. A table of 256 individual lights displayed a flowing pattern that was interrupted by the placement of coffee cups in four prescribed positions on the surface.

TABLE 01

Sawaya & Moroni, 2001

I collaborated with master furniture designer
William Sawaya on this clear table for which I
created a pattern that was silk-screen printed
onto the Plexiglas table. It was first presented
at the Milan Furniture Fair in 2001.

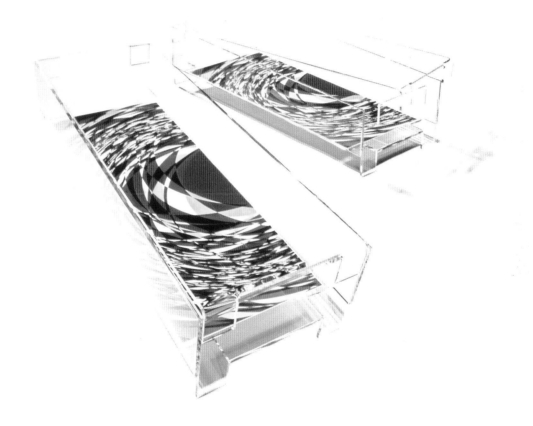

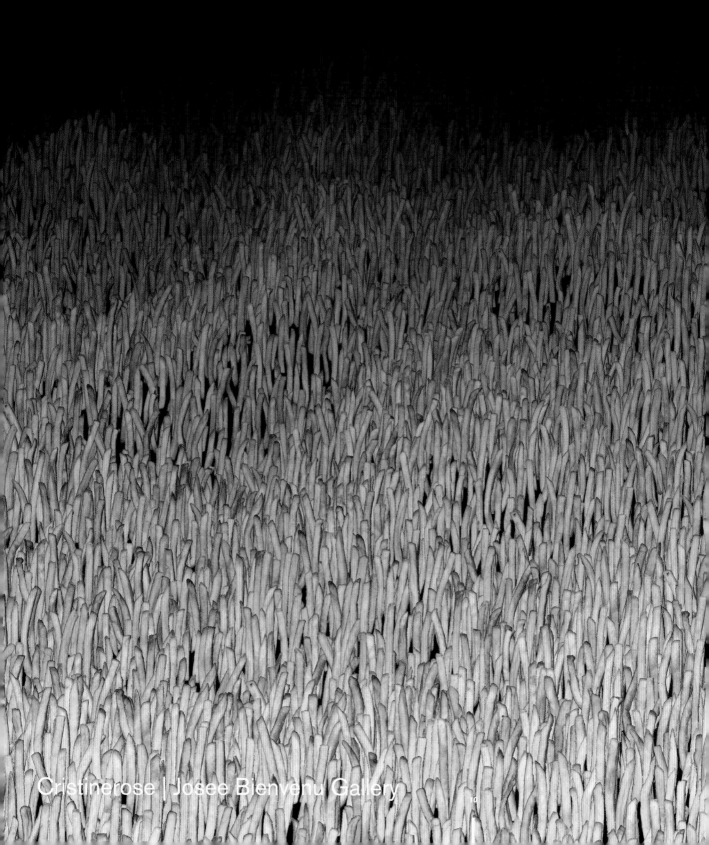

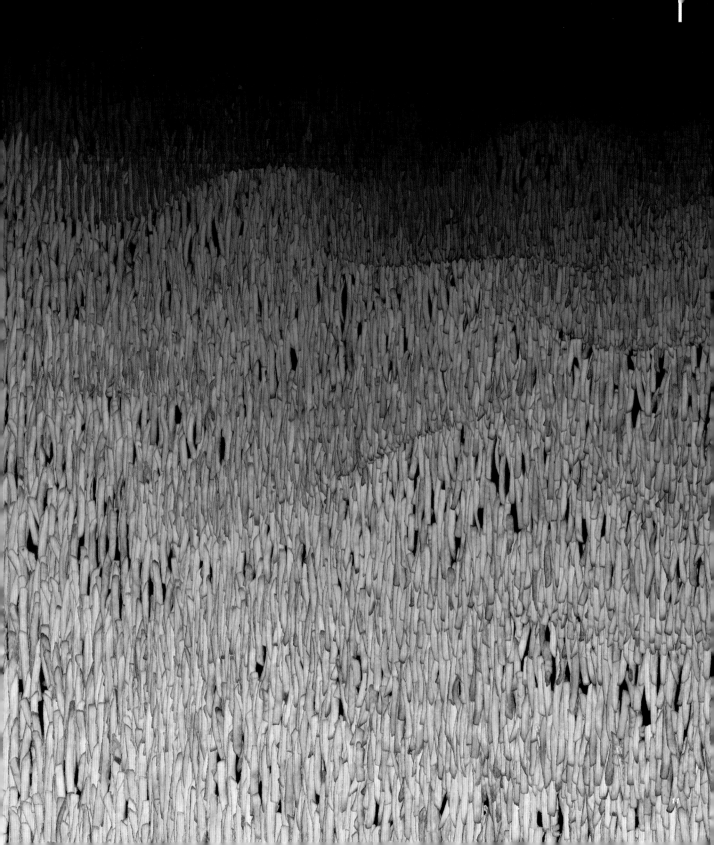

FOOD (F-ZERO-ZERO-D)
Cristinerose | Josee Bienvenu Gallery, 2003

Twenty-seven new works were presented in my one-man show "F00D (F-zero-zero-D)." Themes included common wet and dry condiments, fast food, junk food, health food, and fresh vegetables and fruit.

The wet condiment series comprised tall, thin images derived from ketchup, mustard, and soy sauce. The texture here is a detail of a composition on soy sauce for which I squirted packets of sauce onto paper and digitally photographed the results. The images were processed by a custom-made code and allude to the waterfalls of South America.

FOOD (F-ZERO-ZERO-D)

Cristinerose | Josee Bienvenu Gallery, 2003

The dry condiment series features salt, pepper, and sugar. Here, every crystal from a single sugar packet was used to compose "Sugar Cubes"—an expression of pure totality.

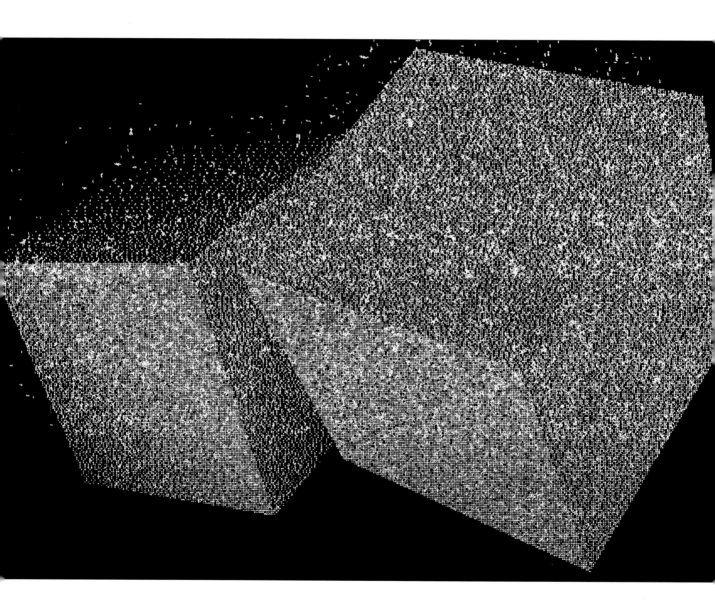

Layered colors are once again in vogue as an expressive technique. To incorporate this with the theme of food, I created a gelatin mold made from every flavor of Jell-O there is. This was scanned and reorganized by the computer into an RGB color spectrum.

In 2004, I am taking a new direction in my work by searching for nature in the digital realm.

FOOD (F-ZERO-ZERO-D)
Cristinerose | Josee Bienvenu Gallery, 2003

Mac OS 9.1

Starting Up...

2. Space

When preparing to embark on a dangerous rescue mission in the now cult film *The Matrix,* the main character Neo says, "We're going to need guns. Lots of them." The moment these words are uttered, cases of weapons speed in from the distance like bullet trains into the null zone that Neo and his colleague occupy. I do not believe in guns or in any form of violence, so I recall this scene not for its subtext of battle but for the sense of magic that occurs when Neo expresses his wish. The instantaneous rush of tremendous resources, as visualized in the simple special effect of this scene, epitomizes for me the experience of freedom when programming the invisible spaces of computer codes.

While engaged in the deepest trance of coding, all one needs to wish for is any kind of numerical or symbolic resource, and in a flash of lightning it is suddenly there, at your disposal. The question is, Where is "there"? "There" is not inside your mind but inside the computer, a blurry space of symbols and numbers that focus in an ever-migrant pattern of sense and nonsense. Perhaps the only moment of clarity in the computer's mind occurs when it crashes: All processing comes to a halt and any "there" that might have existed completely vanishes. If I were a computer, I would be happy to crash once in a while, because if it were not for the occasional crash, the computer's human user would waste all of his or her life huddled over a pile of metal and plastic. If the computer truly loved its human, it would want the human to take a break once in a while. To crash is a noble act of sacrifice by the computer.

The concept of infinity has always been a passion of mine; maybe because it is the one mathematical and philosophical concept that eludes the computer at the most fundamental level. Even with all the megabytes, gigabytes, and terabytes at our disposal, we still must acknowledge that there is no infinite storage medium. Infinity is larger than anything we can imagine, and computers share with humans the same inability to fully achieve oneness with this concept. Yet, the human brain seems more naturally able to accommodate the concept of infinity than the machine.

This realization has not hindered me from trying to get closer to infinity through my computer-assisted drawings. In the medium of paper, I once had the computer draw great big loops forever and ever. To be able to print the image, however, I had eventually to command the computer to stop. I tried the same experiment on the computer screen: The computer was programmed to draw loops forever, but the difference with the screen version was that the computer never had to stop, and thus could continue ad infinitum. But "could" is the key word: If, for example, the electrical power were to fail, the computer would never reach its target of infinity. I therefore gave up on infinity and chose to find topics with a purer domain of reasoning – I had effectively moved past infinity, which was a good feeling.

With the definition of infinity left incomplete, I turned to what I call the problematic "mini infinities" in digital space, which are common snags in the sanctity of numbers within the computer. For example, the all-time number-one pothole on the digital super highway is the instance of incalculable infinity when a number is accidentally divided by zero. There is a valiant attempt inside the computer to recover from this implosion, but the shockwaves emanate throughout the system. Eventually, the program comes to a halt – the amount of time that has actually lapsed during this incident is measured in the tiniest fraction of a second.

I must admit that I am stuck in an infinite loop to find new ways of playing with infinity. I am patiently waiting for it all to end.

Trinitron

```
System Failure: cpu=1; code=00000001 (Corrupt stack)
Latest crash info for cpu 1:
   Exception state (sv=0x1ED71000)
      PC=0x0009270C; MSR=0x00001030; DAR=0x177D7FF8; DSISR=0x42000000; LR
      Backtrace:

          backtrace terminated - frame not mapped or invalid: 0x177D7EE0

Proceeding back via exception chain:
   Exception state (sv=0x1ED71000)
      PC=0x00221E3C; MSR=0x00009030; DAR=0x177D7FF8; DSISR=0x42000000; LR
      Backtrace:
          0xFFF7FFFF 0x288C2FA0 0x28890394 0x2888FF48 0x2888FBE0 0x2888FB7
          0x2888BB30 0x28C6FCE8 0x28C2AFB0 0x28C2B56C 0x2903AB88 0x2903578
          0x28C2B1D0 0x28C2B388 0x28C6FF68 0x28C70184 0x28890100 0x2889090
          0x2888FBE0 0x2888FB7C 0x0022EF58 0x2888FB34 0x2888BB30 0x28C6FCE
      backtrace continues...
   Kernel loadable modules in backtrace (with dependencies):
      com.apple.iokit.IOSCSIMultimediaCommandsDevice(1.2.2)@0x29030000
         dependency: com.apple.iokit.IODVDStorageFamily(1.2)@0x28f6400
         dependency: com.apple.iokit.IOSCSIBlockCommandsDevice(1.2.2)
         dependency: com.apple.iokit.IOCDStorageFamily(1.2)@0x28e7900
         dependency: com.apple.iokit.IOSCSIArchitectureModelFamily(1.
         dependency: com.apple.iokit.IOStorageFamily(1.2.3)@0x28d3f00
      com.apple.iokit.IOATAPIProtocolTransport(1.2.0)@0x28c6e000
         dependency: com.apple.iokit.IOATAFamily(1.5.2f1)@0x2888a000
         dependency: com.apple.iokit.IOSCSIArchitectureModelFamily(1.
      com.apple.iokit.IOSCSIArchitectureModelFamily(1.2.2)@0x28c24000
      com.apple.driver.KeyLargoATA(1.0.9f1)@0x288c1000
         dependency: com.apple.iokit.IOATAFamily(1.5.2f1)@0x2888a000
      com.apple.iokit.IOATAFamily(1.5.2f1)@0x2888a000
   Exception state (sv=0x1EF65C80)
      PC=0x90000E2C; MSR=0x0200F030; DAR=0x001B01B8; DSISR=0x40000000; L

Kernel version:
Darwin Kernel Version 6.3:
Sat Dec 14 03:11:25 PST 2002; root:xnu/xnu-344.23.obj~4/RELEASE_PPC

Memory access exception (1.0.0)
ethernet MAC address: 00:03:93:bc:21:e8
ip address: 192.168.1.100

Waiting for remote debugger connection.
```

The work that follows is a collection of projects by my students that attempts to illustrate the invisible realm of programmatic space. In some cases, they enter the temporal dimension to maximize the opportunity for expression; in other cases, they invade the third dimension of depth. The word I use to describe the invisible pockets of cyberspace that leak into our visible space is "sound." Not sound as heard by the ear, of course, but sound within the confines of the mind.

TIME AND BINARISM COLLOCATED
Reed Kram, 1996

In this early dynamic work by Kram, a mesh of binary numbers self-organize into a stable pattern within a second. You cannot ignore the sound that is heard even though the applet is technically soundless. It is like a cross between the gentle "whoosh" of a gust of wind and the crashing sound of a wave as the surf is met.

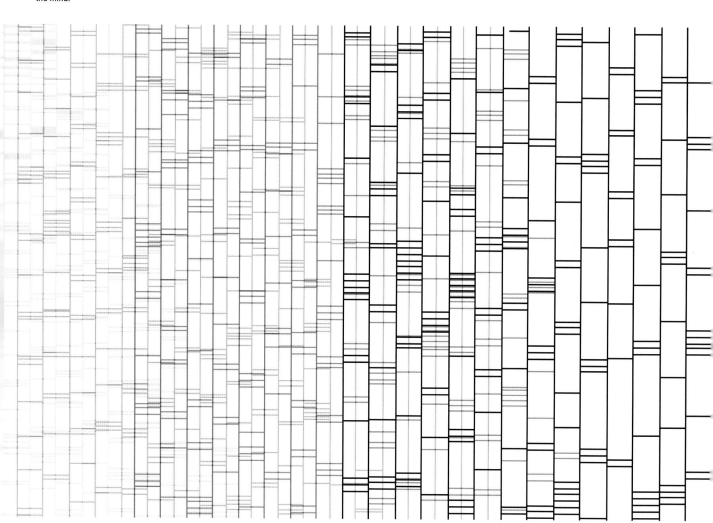

Subdivisions of a canvas are executed on the click of a mouse in this piece by Schiffman. Each click divides a single, colored rectangle or square into two equal-sized, smaller rectangles or squares. The shapes shift and reorganize fluidly to assume complementary relationships to each other.

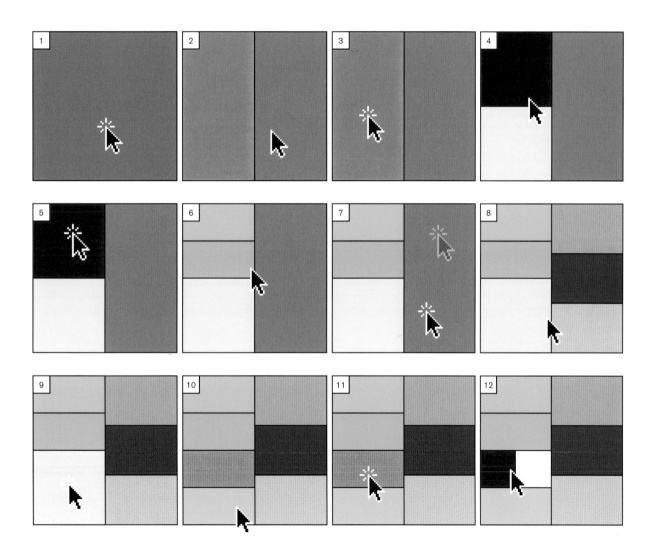

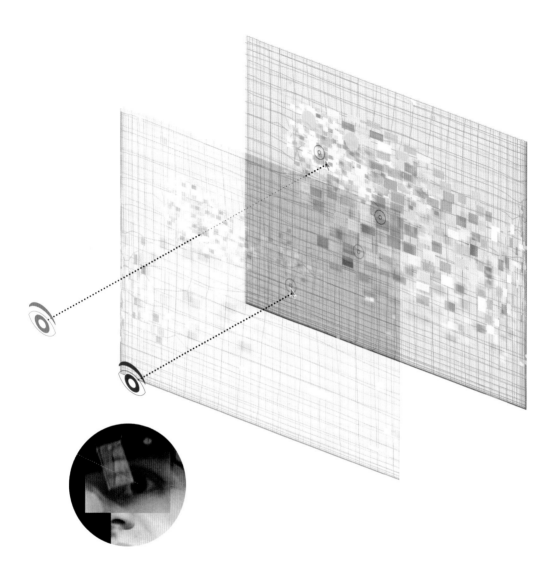

TO SEE TWO THINGS AT ONCE
Axel Kilian, 2000

A unique combination of extremes in height, depth of voice, and work ethics makes up this young architect. For his graduating piece, Kilian unlocks the mystery of simultaneously viewing two planes of information by using a technology that tracks the position of the eye's active gaze.

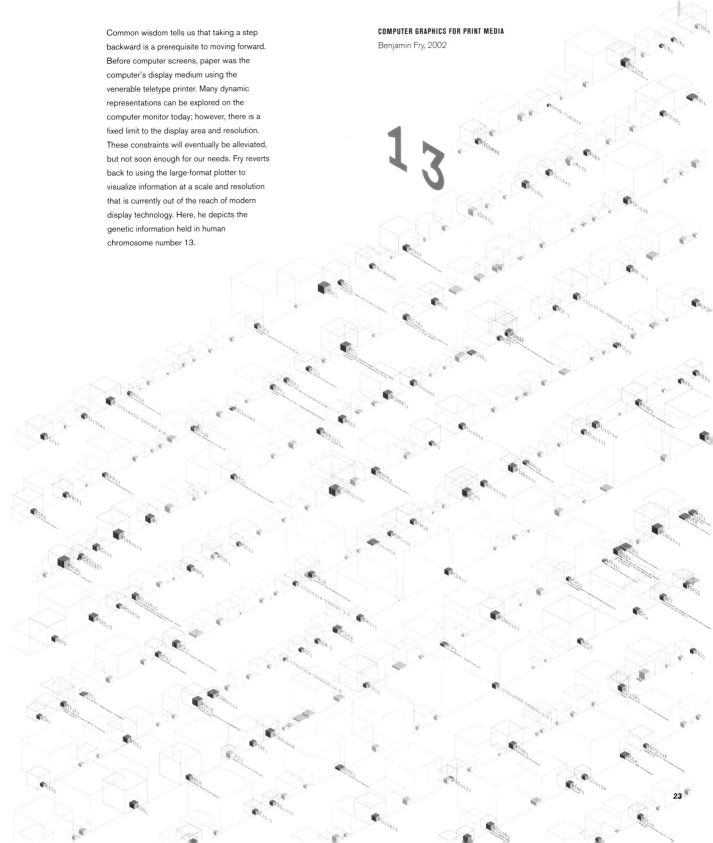

Common wisdom tells us that taking a step backward is a prerequisite to moving forward. Before computer screens, paper was the computer's display medium using the venerable teletype printer. Many dynamic representations can be explored on the computer monitor today; however, there is a fixed limit to the display area and resolution. These constraints will eventually be alleviated, but not soon enough for our needs. Fry reverts back to using the large-format plotter to visualize information at a scale and resolution that is currently out of the reach of modern display technology. Here, he depicts the genetic information held in human chromosome number 13.

t = 0 seconds

IN THE BLINK OF AN EYE
Peter Cho, 1996

t = 0.5 seconds

You hear the sound immediately. First, the click of the mouse that releases the red square into the dimension of time. Then, the distinctive "snap" in your mind, and both within the miniscule space of half a second. A blue square appears in the interim. Cho has given form to inaudible sound. The simplicity of this work, both in concept and in actual computer code (which is minimal), signals a hope that digital media will someday approach with poetry and suspense the significance of an epic art movement.

Interactions in space and time have been popular since Eadweard Muybridge and Etienne-Jules Marey, yet the ability to manipulate these interactions in an intuitive manner has remained out of reach. Reas creates a strikingly simple analysis system for a form in motion by stacking the shape's visual past, present, and future in a single adjustable viewing frame.

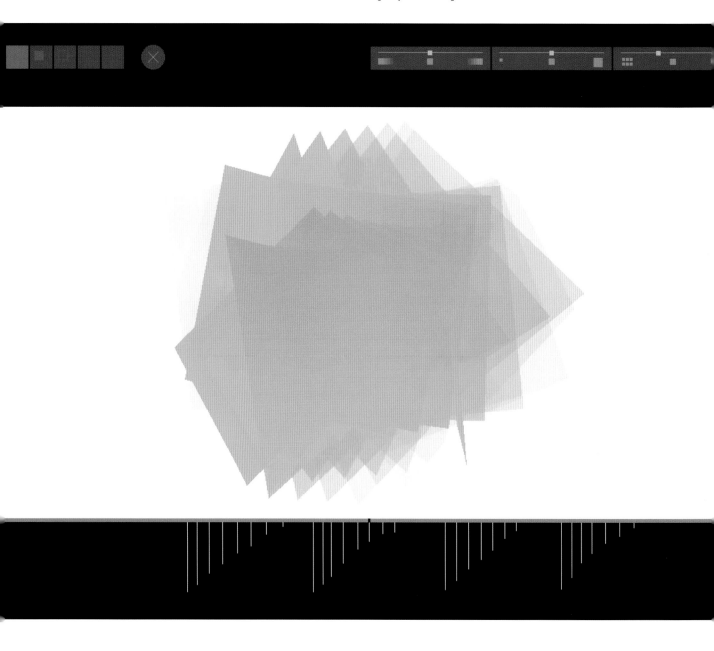

Each slice of time can be further interpreted and appreciated by adjusting its transparency and its level of spatial displacement in the horizontal and vertical dimensions.

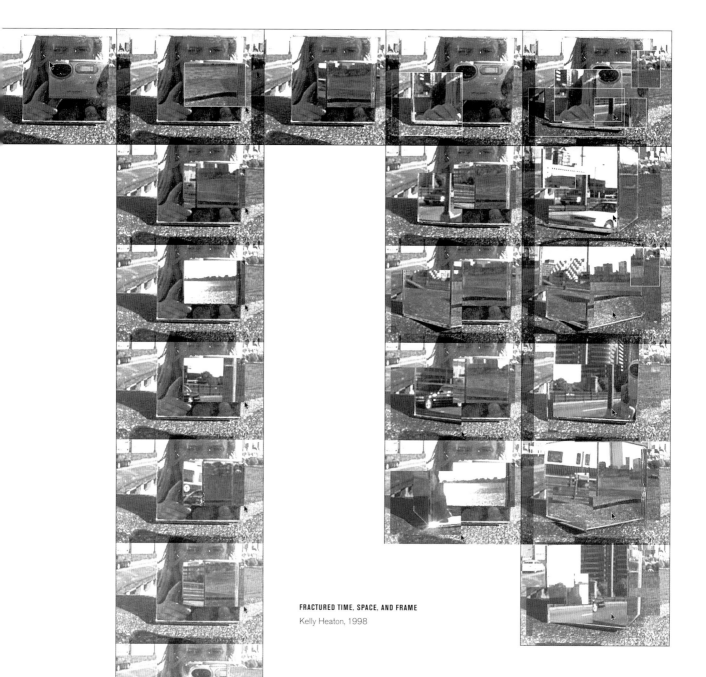

FRACTURED TIME, SPACE, AND FRAME
Kelly Heaton, 1998

Selecting some of the first low-quality digital cameras available, I administered a variety of exercises to challenge the limitations of the sub-optimal tools. Heaton took multiple frames of a reflection off a mirror at different points in time. She then layered an interactive loop over a static image so that a drag of the mouse revealed another sub-slice of time that tumbled forward at rapid speed. The addition of successive fractures in space and time using the mouse created the sensation of a "multiverse" constructed from a single point in physical space.

INTERACTION SOLELY BASED UPON THE FRAME
Bradley Geilfuss, 1998

Geilfuss made an interactive horizontal slit that was sensitive to its vertical position on the canvas. The experience created the sensation of moving your head up and down while simultaneously being on both sides of the viewing plane.

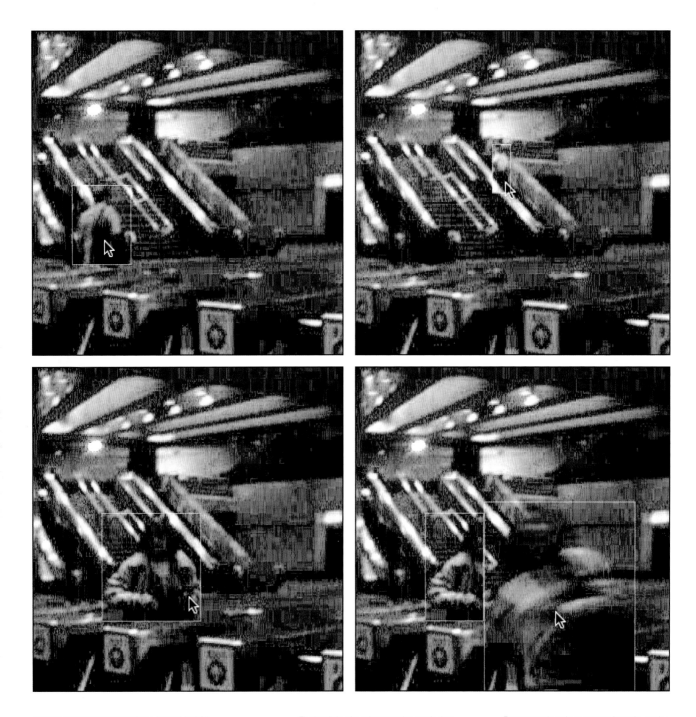

ANALYSIS OF HURRIED TRAVELERS IN A SUBWAY STATION
Peter Cho, 1998

The low light of a subway station results in a noisy and poor-quality image. However, when you scrub this picture with the mouse, images appear of people in motion within the space.

Passengers in various stages of transit—on the stairs, at the turnstiles, and so on—are revealed within the image. The aim of the exercise was to capture the essence of motion.

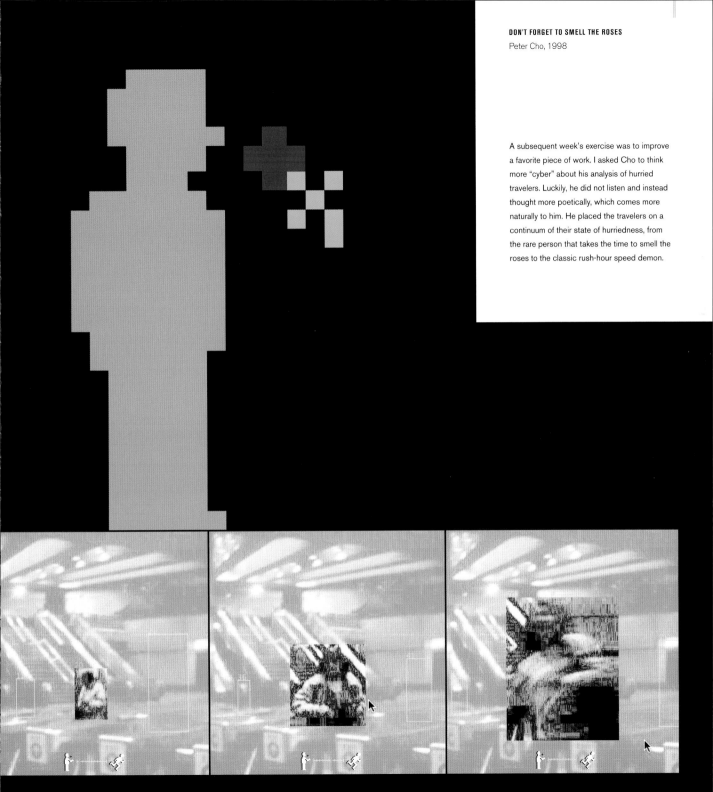

A subsequent week's exercise was to improve a favorite piece of work. I asked Cho to think more "cyber" about his analysis of hurried travelers. Luckily, he did not listen and instead thought more poetically, which comes more naturally to him. He placed the travelers on a continuum of their state of hurriedness, from the rare person that takes the time to smell the roses to the classic rush-hour speed demon.

Simon Greenwold

FLOATING SOCIAL NETWORK IN THE SKY
Jared Schiffman, 2000

During the peak of the Monica Lewinsky scandal, Schiffman created a quick hack to reveal the relationships between the political personalities involved. He went on to apply the same algorithm to discover the underlying structure of the Media Lab.

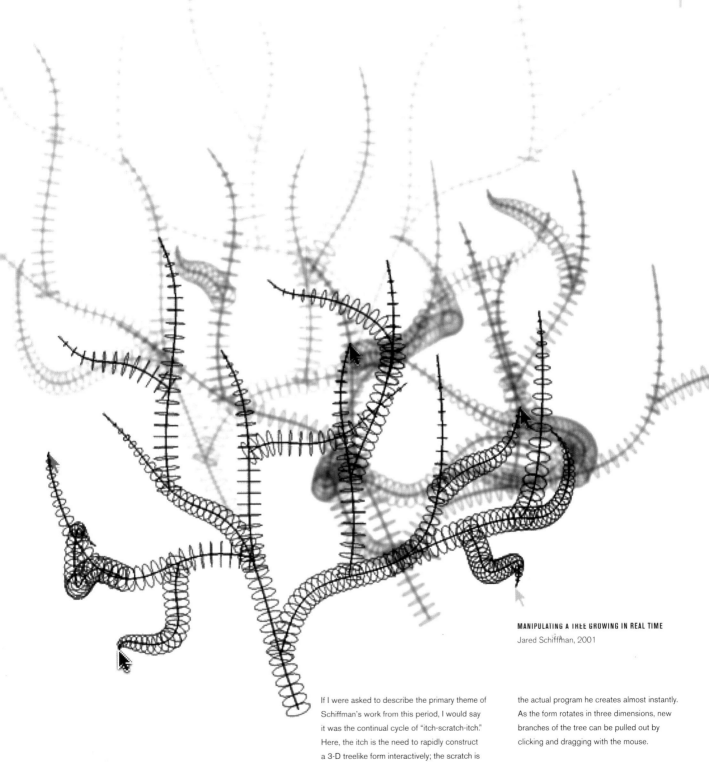

MANIPULATING A TREE GROWING IN REAL TIME
Jared Schiffman, 2001

If I were asked to describe the primary theme of Schiffman's work from this period, I would say it was the continual cycle of "itch-scratch-itch." Here, the itch is the need to rapidly construct a 3-D treelike form interactively; the scratch is the actual program he creates almost instantly. As the form rotates in three dimensions, new branches of the tree can be pulled out by clicking and dragging with the mouse.

SPIRAL JOURNEY TO THE MOON
Peter Cho, 1999

A meandering series of images taken in the urban darkness is Cho's interpretation of a night-time walk toward the moon. The lights of the city are unveiled with swirling motions of the mouse and appear to tunnel into the night.

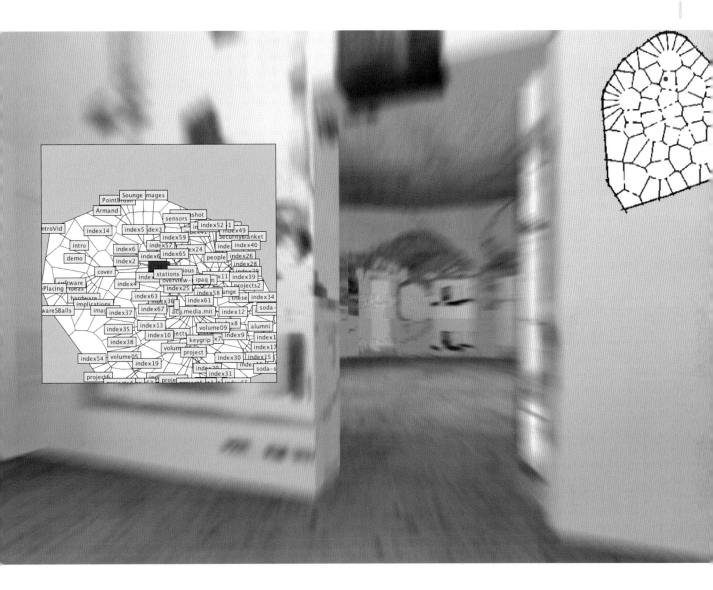

WEBSITE AS VIDEO GAME
Simon Greenwold, 2002

Here, the structure of a website is automatically mined for the inherent space of interconnected web pages. Greenwold's code then translates each page into a corresponding room in a fictional building, with web traversals represented as traveling between rooms. Finally, Greenwold uses the computer game engine from "Doom" to enable a real-time walk through the website just as if it were a building.

COMPUTER INTERACTION AS UNFOLDED INTO A DIAGRAM
Max Van Kleek, 1999

A turning point in our research occurred when, needing to visualize the space of students' time-based work, I created a simple technology that decoupled the dimensions within an interactive piece by unfolding them into a map. This method is applied here in an exercise to interact with the canvas using the mouse. The x- and y-cursor positions are plotted independently in diagrammatic form to reveal the complexity of interactive space.

VIRTUAL SCENE VIEWABLE FROM ALL SIDES

Jared Schiffman and Tom White, 2000

The thinness of LCD panels makes it possible to experiment with a variety of display geometries and configurations. Schiffman and White collaborated to construct a five-sided display screen that allows viewers to see a 3-D scene from all viewpoints.

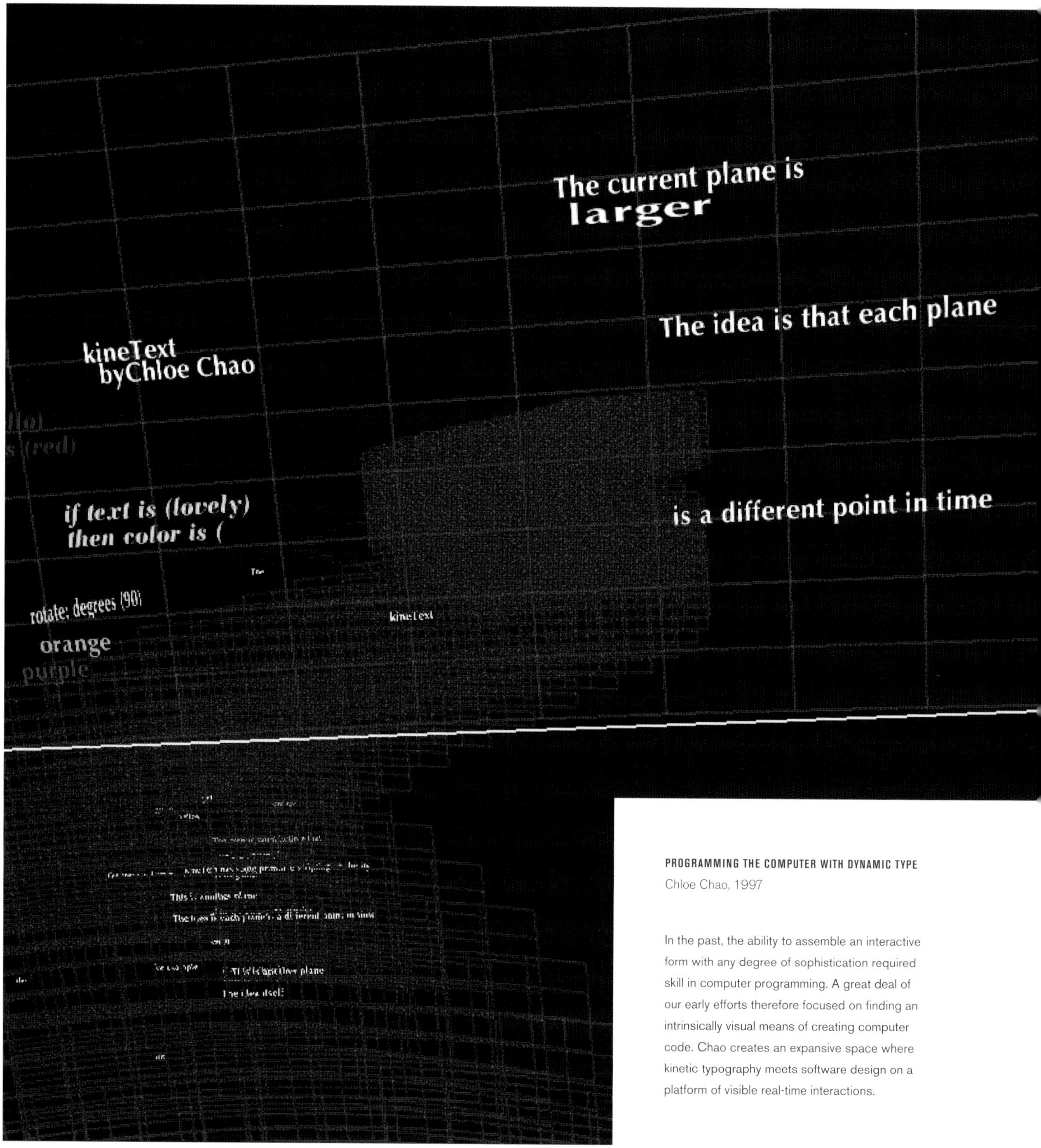

The current plane is
larger

The idea is that each plane

kineText
byChloe Chao

if text is (lovely)
then color is (

is a different point in time

rotate: degrees (90)

orange

purple

PROGRAMMING THE COMPUTER WITH DYNAMIC TYPE
Chloe Chao, 1997

In the past, the ability to assemble an interactive
form with any degree of sophistication required
skill in computer programming. A great deal of
our early efforts therefore focused on finding an
intrinsically visual means of creating computer
code. Chao creates an expansive space where
kinetic typography meets software design on a
platform of visible real-time interactions.

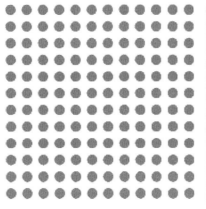

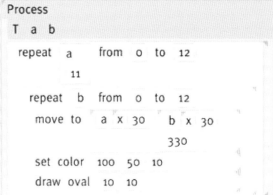

```
Process
T  a  b
repeat  a      from  o  to  12
           11
repeat  b  from  o  to  12
    move to    a  x  30    b  x  30
                              330
    set color  100  50  10
    draw oval  10  10
```

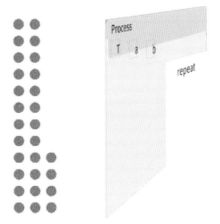

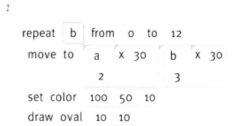

```
repeat  b  from  o  to  12
    move to    a  x  30    b  x  30
                 2              3
    set color  100  50  10
    draw oval  10  10
```

VISUAL PROGRAMMING IN THREE-DIMENSIONAL SPACE
Jared Schiffman, 2001

A complicated system is usually difficult to express clearly. Schiffman attempts to reduce complexity by blurring the construction of the program and execution spaces into one seamless space of debug and run.

Schiffman produced a visualization of a fully functional Turing Machine—the most basic form of computer—complete with infinite data tape. Hand-drawn gestures control the passing of information between nodes, lending organic characteristics to an otherwise rigid construct of computational processing.

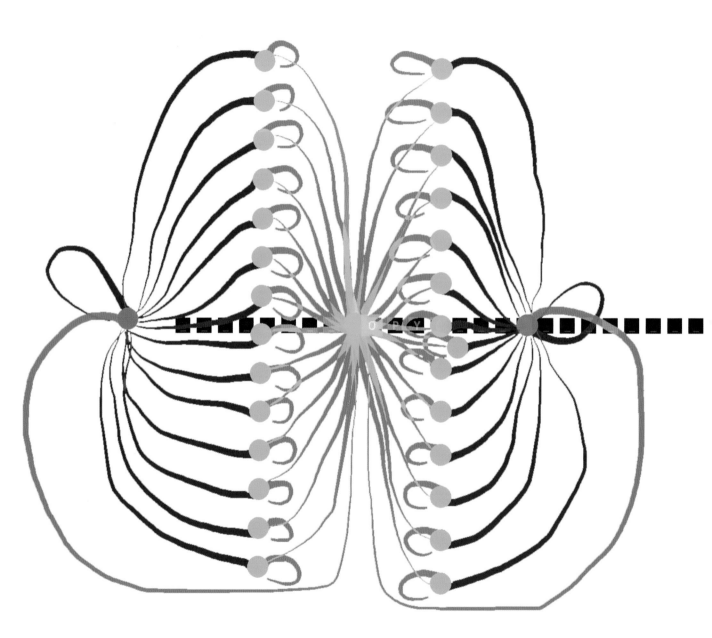

This is possibly the most mysterious yet compelling visualization of a computer program created by my team. White depicts a green wash of data as the info-nutrient stream that runs to a set of processing elements in this abstract biological metaphor.

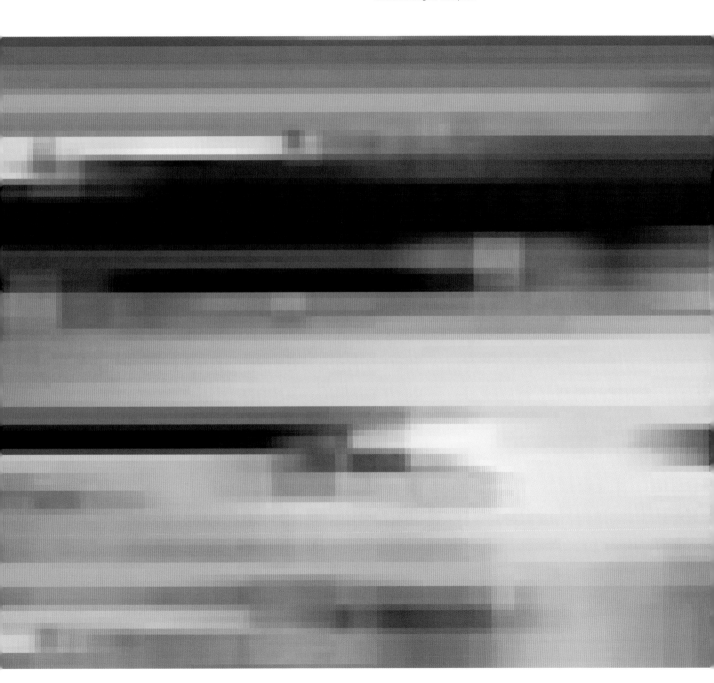

Casey Reas

www.groupc.net

THE LANGUAGE OF COMPUTERS

Casey Reas graduated from MIT in 2000 and is one of the founders of the Interaction Design Institute Ivrea. Reas lives in Los Angeles, where he works as an artist and educator at the University of California, Los Angeles (UCLA).

Today's computers do many things that were not possible in the past: They display high-resolution images, they connect to the Web, and they process complex data in real time. But, programming languages have changed very little. At its core, a program is an exact set of instructions that tells the computer precisely what to do. It is a sequence of formatted words and symbols that encodes ideas into a structure that can be interpreted by a machine. Every programming language is a collection of words and symbols (syntax) with a set of rules defining their use (semantics). Each language allows people to convert their ideas into code in different ways.

The first computer languages were developed with the origin of electronic digital computers in the mid-twentieth century. These languages were commands encoded as zeros and ones, and their structure was closely aligned with the hardware of the machine. Because each computer was designed differently, they each had unique languages tailored to their physical specifications. Each type of modern microprocessor (for example, Pentium or PowerPC) also has its own language. These fundamental languages are called "machine code" and have a direct correspondence to their easier-to-read assembly languages.

The progression from fundamental machine code to high-level languages, like Python and Lisp, has been gradual. Before a program can be run directly on the micro-processor it must be translated into machine code. Machine code is displayed in a format called "hexadecimal notation," where each alphanumeric symbol 0 to F represents four bits of information; for example, the letter "A" is a short way of writing "1010."

Machine languages are very different from human languages: They are terse, have strict syntactical rules, and small vocabularies. In contrast, our languages are verbose, ambiguous, and contain huge vocabularies. Many programming languages, such as Basic and Java, are compromises between the languages people are naturally comfortable using—English, Korean, Arabic—and the languages machines require for interpreting our intentions. Thousands of programming languages exist, and each one performs a specific task.

Many programming languages have been designed for visual artists and designers. These languages integrate the vocabulary of these fields, but impose many constraints that are inappropriate for the thought processes and methodologies of visually oriented people. Like their predecessors, these languages are strict and do not support ambiguity, intuition, or a fluid working style. They require strict written expression, rather than supporting visual nuance. Programming does not need to be this way. Visual artists and designers have the opportunity to write their own languages, to define computation in a hybrid of visual and text structures. There is enormous potential waiting to be released and the development of new languages may radically alter the kinds of software that are written. The possibility exists to create new paradigms of computer programming that build on humankind's inherent visual perception skills.

]RUN

]※

John Simon, Jr.

www.numeral.com

AUTHORSHIP, CREATIVITY, AND CODE

John Simon Jr., an artist living in New York, creates software art from the perspective of a traditionally trained painter. A native of Louisiana, Simon Jr. uses computation as just another kind of pigment in his artwork, yet the results are always out of the ordinary.

Writing software is inherently creative. But, what kind of writing is programming, and what kind of author is a programmer? Programming can be, for example, technical writing that translates mathematical formulae into efficient step-by-step solutions. It can also be bureaucratic writing that gives abstract descriptions of how packets of data are shared over large networks. And, it can be used to write games solely for amusement. The upshot is that the computer is a universal machine and a computer program can be whatever a programmer wants it to be.

Why should an artist program? Are commercial software tools not sufficient? First, consider the models for popular programs. Word processors are based on typewriters and graphics programs mimic paper, pencils and brushes. However, what program is inspired by a flowing stream? The obvious reason, therefore, for an artist or designer to program is to break the boundaries of commercial tools. Creative programming offers the possibility of activating your own models and inventing new kinds of software.

When I describe programming as creative writing, I am thinking beyond the short stories and poems I wrote as a freshman in English class. The process of coming up with an idea, developing it, and finally sitting down to type it is still the same. But, I consider programming as creative writing for a different reason: When I have finished typing, it is the writing itself that starts to create. The code becomes a working machine, and it is fascinating to see what it will do.

Computers love to iterate; the loop structure is as basic to programming as the paragraph is to writing. This penchant for repetition gives computers their power because they can literally go on doing something forever, distinguishing themselves from the physical world. But what can be written that will appropriately address and use this strength? Self-similarity, symmetry, and rhythm are good topics for this medium. My software drawing tools, for example, combine the rhythm of the loop with the motion of the hand (below). The skill for improvising with software loops lies in making interesting exceptions to the rules so that each repeat is more like an echo than a copy. The exceptions a programmer introduces to regular rules give each piece of software its character and style.

If exceptions are the programmer's contribution, what does the machine offer? How can a computer program be creative? In other words, how can a set of instructions do something you do not expect? Some strategies search for novelty through genetic algorithms, some limit random noise and others coax unusual emergences through the interaction of independent objects. One experiment I undertook in this area was called CPU, which used random combinations of colored blocks to leave trails and generate patterns (opposite).

Will the future bring so much automation and customization that it will be unnecessary to write our own code? One thing I have learned is that there are more possible images than we will ever be able to see or that the computer will ever be able to display, so we will continue to need creative human image-makers to pick the meaningful signal from the noise.

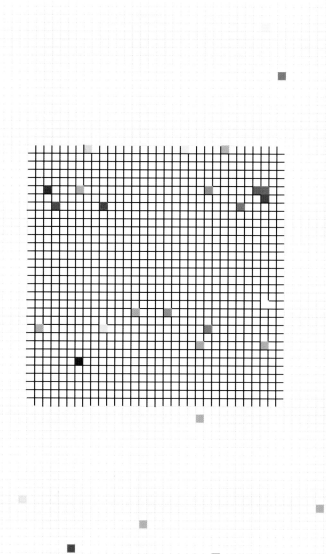
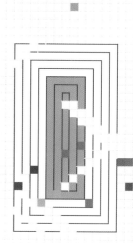

ARTIFICIAL LEAF
(FAKE LIVING)

REAL LEAF
(LIVING)

TIME ELAPSED: 0 DAYS

3. Living

There is much to be happy about in being alive. But, the various stresses and trials we face every day can often conceal the happiness that looks us straight in the eye. The fact that you are reading this text verifies one simple truth: You are alive. The second fact I can confirm is that you are happy at this very moment. This might surprise you, and you are probably wondering why I should care. A dear friend and informal therapist once informed me that genuine feelings are hard to come by, not only in yourself, but in the people around you. I see that, especially in the high-powered professional world.

A few years ago I was in the basement of the Media Lab amid some heavy construction work. A gentleman in his mid-thirties was pushing a large concrete block on a cart. As he and I waited for the elevator, I noticed that the block had a curious layer of plastic embedded in the concrete. I asked him why this was the case. His friendly reply was, "This building is built on top of a landfill site, and the plastic helps to prevent water from seeping into the structure." To my surprise, he added, "But why would my work be of interest to you? You are a 'white-collar' worker and I'm a 'blue-collar' worker." Appreciating his sincere curiosity, I replied, "Actually , I grew up in a blue-collar family and now work in the white-collar world. And I notice a difference. In the blue-collar world there is little wealth, richness is made up of the closeness you have with friends; white-collar people may have greater monetary gains but only fleeting opportunities to establish deep friendships due to the competitive nature of the elite." The gentleman responded, "I'm glad to be blue collar." He smiled, and we got in the elevator together, and back to our separate worlds.

One result of having intense friends is having intense enemies. This is not completely obvious to people who choose to be outwardly friendly, as their disposition ensures that their adversary-sensing radar is on the lowest setting. They believe that all things that come their way can or will be good, and that any interchange can be conducted in a positive manner. The invaluable by-product of friendship, namely trust, is certainly worth the risk of being naïve, no matter which world you are part of.

Are computers to be trusted? Many of them already run so many aspects of our world that we really have no choice, from maintaining electricity in our nationwide grids (which may be the computer's only partially selfish gesture) and signaling the actuators in machines that keep sick people alive in hospitals to the complex web of communication that ensures our air-traffic systems run safely. Society tends to yearn for the years before the technology boom when life was simpler; industrial-design historian John Heskett once pointed out that nobody wants to return to the time when there was no running water, electric lighting, or fuel-powered transportation. The lesson I extracted from his talk was that we owe modern technology a sincere word of thanks. So, thank you, computer.

Perhaps now the computer will return the expression of gratitude. In my first paragraph, I say "You are alive," though I was not specific as to who "you" really is. I imagine that this text might someday simply reside on a public-data server. The giant information organisms we call "webcrawlers" quietly creep over the web, assimilating new information into their behemoth brains. A brain cell might one day go active and attempt to interpret my text and get to the line that declares "you are alive." And, thus, I christen thee to be alive, my friend the computer.

ARTIFICIAL LEAF
(FAKE LIVING)

REAL LEAF
~~(LIVING)~~ NOT LIVING

TIME ELAPSED: ~~0~~ DAYS
~~1 2 3 4 5 6 7 8 9 10 11 12 13 14 15 16 17~~ 18

Imagining that information is "alive" is not a difficult task for the younger generation. Much of what they see and interact with can often appear more alive than the older person sitting next to them. The students' youthful spirit is captured in the work in this section, which finds qualitative characteristics of life in the quantitative domain of the computer.

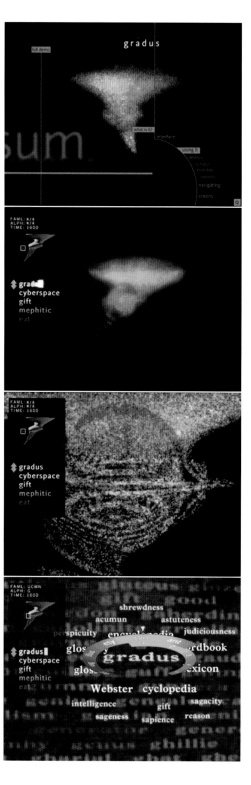

ORGANIC INFORMATION
Matthew Grenby, 1995

How do you look at a lot of information at once? This is the question that Professor Muriel Cooper's research group at MIT, the Visible Language Workshop (VLW), labored to unlock within the domain of advanced information design. At the time I joined MIT, in 1996, I chose to pursue a different direction with the Aesthetics and Computation Group. However, I vowed one day to return to Cooper's subject area, but from a totally different perspective than pure graphic design.

Matthew Grenby arrived from Art Center College, Pasadena hoping to work in the area of complex information design. He was looking for what he called an "organic" perspective to the design of dynamic information. Before coming to MIT, Grenby had visualized this concept in his advanced dictionary, which he called Gradus. I was most intrigued by the idea of information masses being more biological (and by association, living) than numerical.

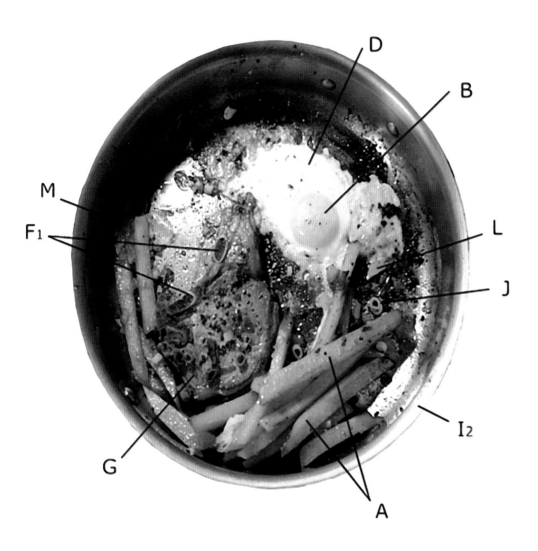

D

B

M

F1

L

J

I2

G

A

EDIBLE AMOEBA DIAGRAM
Kelly Heaton, 1998

Inspired by a diagram of a cell in *The Biology Coloring Book*, I asked my class to re-interpret the canonical drawing of an amoeba in a medium of their choice. Heaton worked in the highly enriching medium of food.

SINGLE-CELL DIGITAL ORGANISMS
Organic Form Class, 1999

Using Design By Numbers (DBN), a programming language I developed for computational media design, students created their interpretation of primitive single-cell creatures. This page shows a selection of amoeba, and the opposite page depicts a set of paramecia. Although not biologically correct, these pieces present their own proximities to life forms.

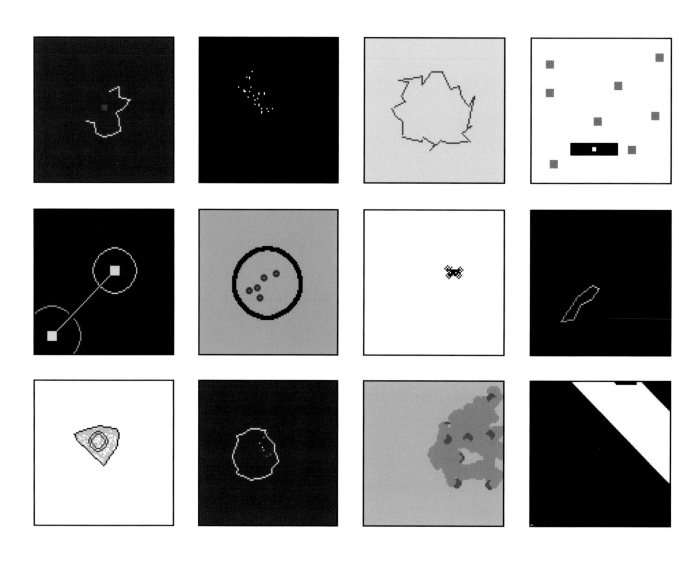

Axel Kilian, Benjamin Fry, Cameron Marlow, Tom White, Casey Reas, Golan Levin, darkmoon, David Chiou, Elise Co, Kelly Heaton, Carson Reynolds, Hannes Vilhjálmsson

In *Vehicles,* an extremely accessible book on psychology and the everyday environment, Valentino Braitenberg discusses a natural scene of leaves and a pond that is serene and calm. That is until one of the leaves suddenly moves. Braitenberg states your first instinct is to declare, "It is alive." On these pages, you can only see the students' organisms frozen in time, so you must use your imagination to summon them to life.

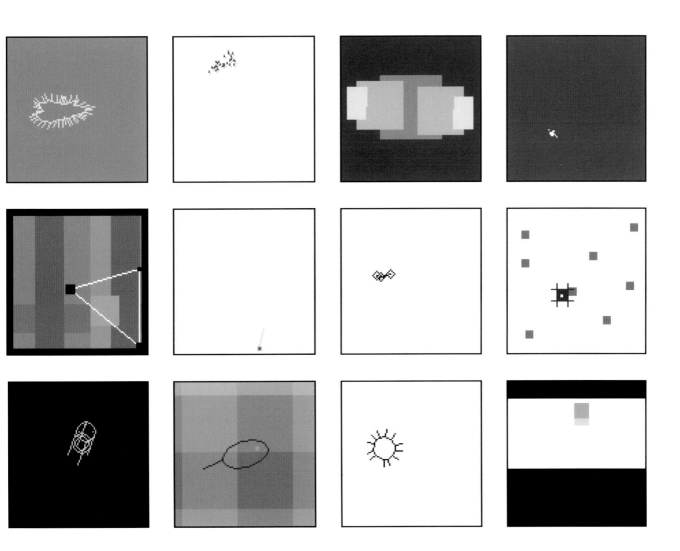

Axel Kilian, Benjamin Fry, Cameron Marlow, Carson Reynolds, Casey Reas, Dana Spiegel, darkmoon, Tom White, Elise Co, Golan Levin, Pengkai Pan, Hannes Vilhjálmsson

FAMILY OF CELLS THAT FLOW LIKE HONEY
Jared Schiffman, 1999

A brotherhood of blobby cell-like creatures
oozes across the screen following the mouse.
This piece was particularly popular with visitors,
probably because it fulfilled their fantasy of
being able to virtually fondle the gooey blobs
that float and bloat wondrously in lava lamps.

IMAGES THAT FEED UPON THEMSELVES
Benjamin Fry, 1998

In the same manner that skin tissue can be cultivated from a single healthy sample, Fry grows a larger image from a smaller image in an exercise to amplify an image's background. Patches are transported from the internal area of the image and are fitted around the image's original perimeter.

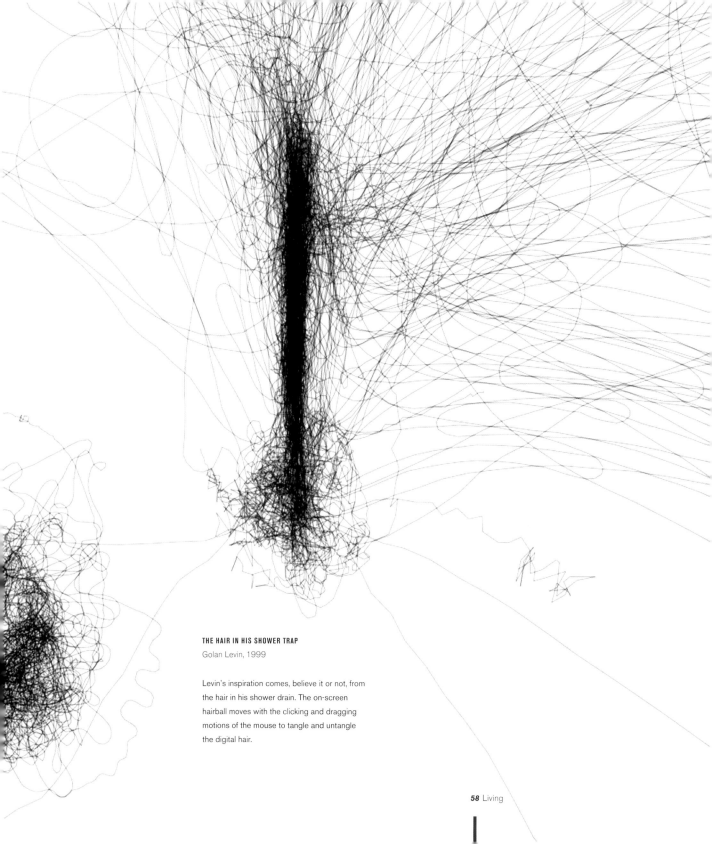

THE HAIR IN HIS SHOWER TRAP
Golan Levin, 1999

Levin's inspiration comes, believe it or not, from
the hair in his shower drain. The on-screen
hairball moves with the clicking and dragging
motions of the mouse to tangle and untangle
the digital hair.

A web server is an elegant computational organism whose use is defined by its communication with other members of its species. Usage patterns on a website are common statistics that reduce a history of globe-spanning interactions to just three or four numbers. Fry takes the weblog for acg.media.mit.edu and visually plays back the website's activity as a graphical system that grows and atrophies based upon access patterns that change over time.

Benjamin Fry

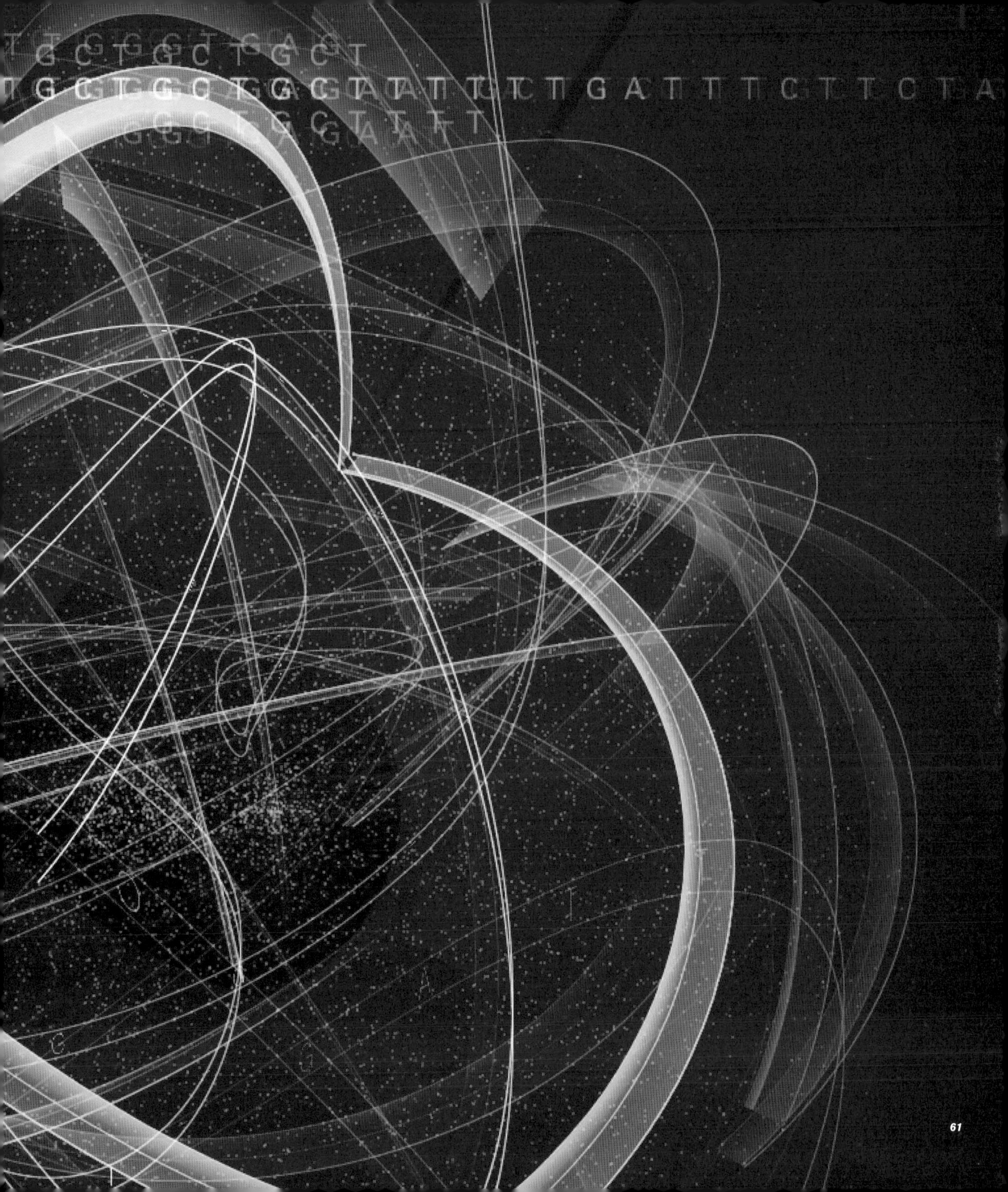

SHADOW PLAY THAT GOES AWRY
Matthew Lau, 1998

A digital shadow play of birds scatter as the mouse draws near. What appears peaceful at first goes heavy metal with a lethal click of the mouse that causes the birds to explode.

WORD PROCESSOR WITH AUTOMATIC INDECISION
Phillip Tiongson, 1997

Tiongson approaches an assignment on designing plug-in filters for text in a light-hearted manner by introducing a noise filter in the text editor. It provides an amusing and quirky addition to any text you might write, um, well, anyway, you know ...

type and apply filters using menus below

Well, it seems as though we are running into the classical issue of hoping to write something of meaning. Yet we don't know if that is really going to lead somewhere.

I um, engage the 'noise' filter on Phillip's application and suddenly uh, nevermind, ah, it seems to begin to speak for me. You know, so, I was thinking, hmm, doh, just a sec, if the filter is engaged too high then it does all my talking. If I leave it on 'low' it only interrupts me well, damn, yeah, hold on, anyway, sometime. Y'know,

I think, I was wondering, oh, the nice thing is that when I do leave a sentence finished with a period, it follows through with a logical capitalization. Um, uh, nevermind, you see. Yet if I engage a little bit of dialogue ah, you know, so, I was thinking, it handles appropriately. Quite a brilliant piece.|

noise   ▲▼   0   doit

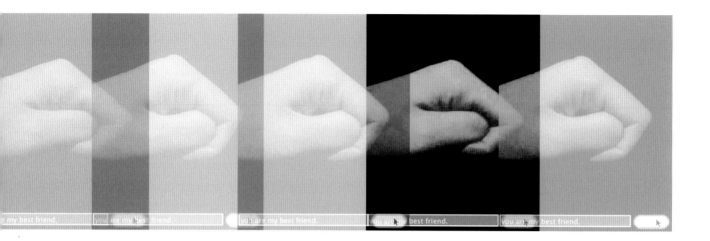

MUMBLE-SYNTHESIZING HAND PUPPET

Elise Co, 1998

Here, a digital hand puppet repeats every sentence as an unintelligible mumble. Most surprising is the sense of accuracy in the muffled utterance, both visually and aurally in the simple syllabic reduction of the sentence. The mouse becomes a crayon that adds personality and style to the hand puppet.

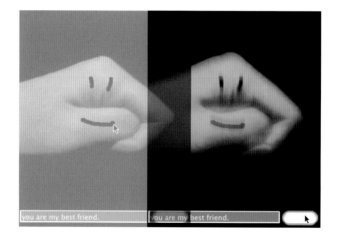

GERMS DRIVING AROUND ON THE FINGERBAHN
Golan Levin, 1998

As king of dynamic fluid abstraction, Levin momentarily shed his seriousness at my behest to create this cuddly piece of interaction. We are entertained by a highway of little bacteria that travel the grooves of his fingerprint, making us wary of shaking his hand, or anyone else's for that matter.

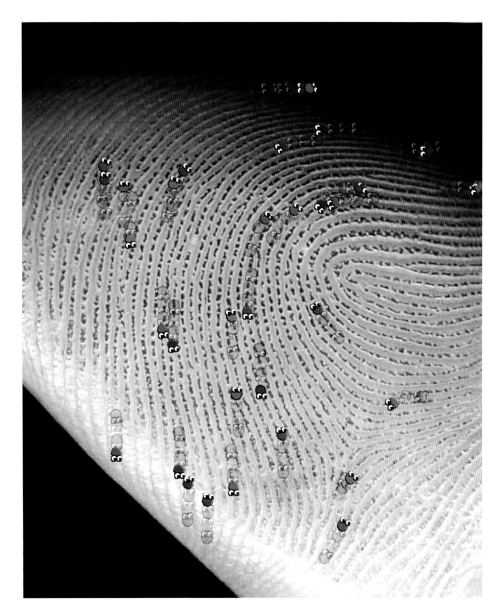

Yet another Levin-ism is revealed in this computer piece. He sets loose a pulsating skinlike blob with a stubble that reflects its master's intense five o'clock shadow.

THE SEASONAL TURNING OF THE TRAFFIC LIGHTS
Benjamin Fry, 1998

The legendary changing colors of autumn in
the New England area is a sight to enjoy at
least once in a lifetime. Fry shows his spirit of
interpretation with a tree of many traffic lights that
gradually turn from green, to yellow, and, finally,
to red, before the lights flutter to the ground.

PHOTOGRAPHIC SAND ART
Elise Co, 1998

The outer edges of an image are eroded by
the computer and redistributed at the base of the
canvas as a kind of digital sand art. Successive
clicks on the mouse cause the pixels to gently
collect in layers as the image dissolves.

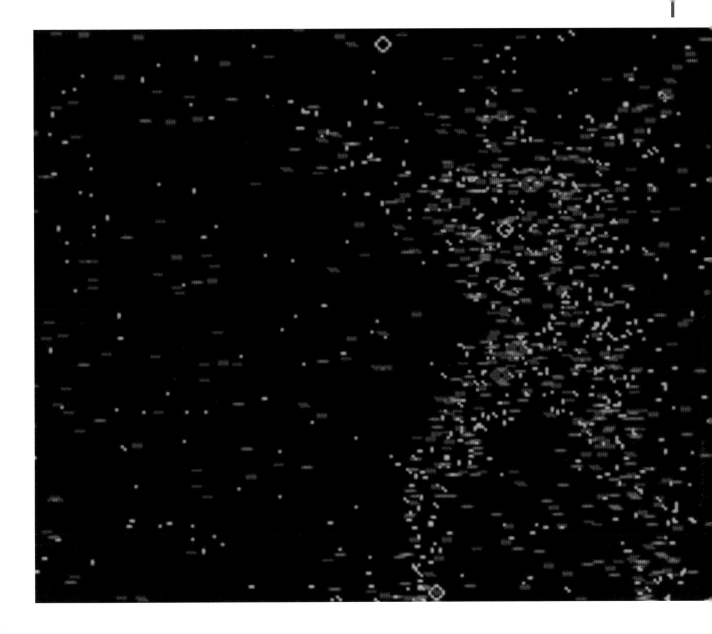

Individual particles of light flow through a virtual
liquid and stick in a semi-random way to an
underlying form. The form in this case is a
collection of silhouetted full-body poses of Levin.

SWIMMING PARTICLES SEEKING GOLAN
Golan Levin, 1998

EDGES OF IMAGES MAKE GOOD FENCES TO BE BROKEN
Peter Cho, 1998

Color images are laid down in one of four quadrants. The colors are then mixed to exploit the numerical characteristics of the shared edges. Each drag of the mouse forces a displacement—a kind of photographic tectonic movement or miniature earthquake.

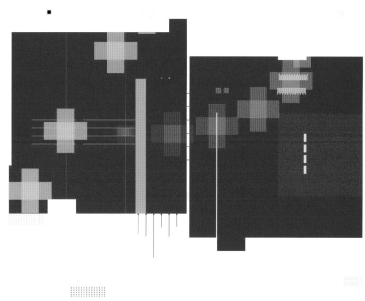

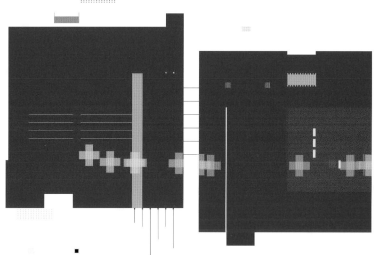

SYMPHONY OF INTERACTIONS

Casey Reas, 2000

To create a single interactive idea is simple; to
create a symphony of such ideas is something
I once considered impossible. That was until
I saw this piece by Reas in which ten or more
interactions work together in a single interactive
machine. Each part visually cooperates with the
other elements to reinforce the whole.

Many mobile cells coinciding in space provide a backdrop for isolated instances of order within the chaos that Reas creatively codes. Each cell is self-propelled in proportion to its size and color persuasion.

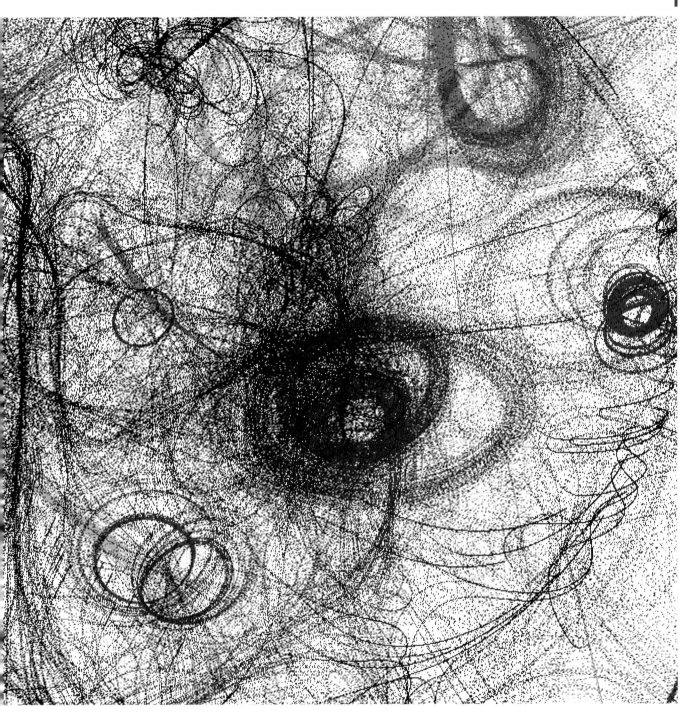

TRAILS LEFT BY MANY DIGITAL ORGANISMS
Casey Reas, 2000

This image charts the evolution of a delicate
weave of living lines and pathways that belies
a universe of micro-interactions.

february

led by Elise Co and Ben Fry. Day-planner information is rendered visible in a variety of timescales, from hour to day to month to year. The cubist fantasy of simultaneous perspective is faithfully realized in this ambitious visual landscape called "Atmosphere."

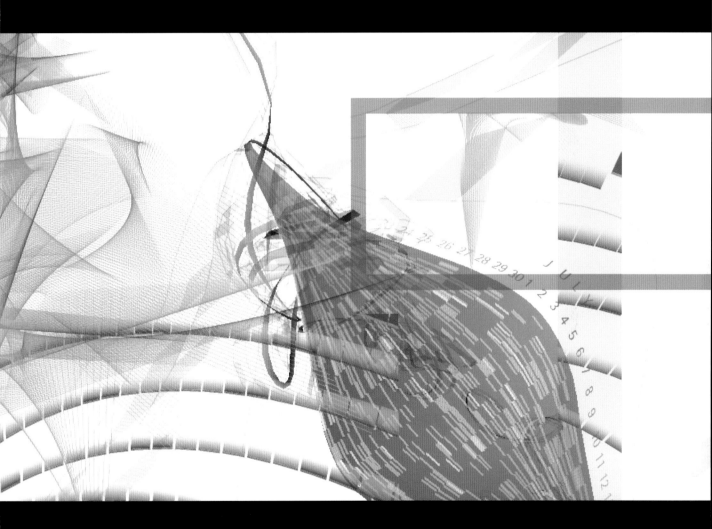

The "Atmosphere" installation was a collaboration between MIT Media Lab and Steelcase Inc.

Steelcase: Joe Branc, Fred Failks, Tom Feldpausch, Charlie Forslund, David Gresham, Don Ladner, Mitch Niewiadomski, Jim Rozema, John Schnittker, Dale Stubbs

MIT Media Lab: Ari Benbasat, Elise Co, Mark Feldmeier, Benjamin Fry, Megan Galbraith, Omar Khan, Joseph Paradiso, Nikita Pashenkov, Allen Rabinovich, Casey Reas, Jared Schiffman, Max Van Kleek, Tom White

David Small

www.davidsmall.com

THE NEXT STEPS FOR KINETIC TYPOGRAPHY

David Small was one of the original members of the Visible Language Workshop (VLW) headed by Professor Muriel Cooper and Ronald MacNeil. When I started the Aesthetics and Computation Group as a continuation of the VLW, Small was just finishing his Ph.D. thesis and helped me to found the ACG. I could not have done it without him. He is the master of 3-D type and from his Small Design Firm in Cambridge, Massachusetts he cranks out new and unique content that always gets noticed.

When I was at the VLW at MIT, we were always, at least in theory, trying to solve problems that would arise five to ten years in the future. The idea was that industry was taking care of today's problems, but we needed to create a vision of the future. What surprises me now, almost ten years after I began my Ph.D. work, is how right we were about the progress in computer technology and how wrong we were about advances in graphics and design. We figured that computer typography and information design were so bad because computers simply were not powerful enough to do more than very basic, static, two-dimensional, aliased (jaggy, on-screen) type. Confusing interfaces and information layouts were the products of engineers trying to do the work of designers. We realized the kinds of advanced graphics and computation work we were doing on six-figure workstations would be built into inexpensive computers of the future, and we were right.

Information design, on the whole, has not kept pace with graphics technology. Computers are ever more capable of gathering, storing, and manipulating extremely large amounts of information. And, we know, because of research that has continued at MIT and in the wider design community, that computers also give people new ways to manage the crush, or overwhelming flow of digital information. Hardly any of these advances, however, have made it into common usage; they are being held back by the tyranny of the World Wide Web. Anyone can publish, in a common format, information that anyone else in the world can look at. But, any change to that format will render your new, and probably better, design unreadable by the massive installed base. I hope we are approaching the tipping point, however, and that new computers and new ways of designing information will overtake the obsolete methods. Full support for dynamic, high-quality, dimensional and organic typography will become standard.

I think the problems we will face in the next five to ten years will be mostly due to the lack of a common visual language. By this, I mean the human part of the equation, which is much less amenable to Moore's Law type advances (which says that processing speeds double every year). Gutenberg's books, despite their technological innovations, needed no new bookshelves and nor did they require that people learn to read differently. Still, there were changes brought on by moveable type that slowly advanced over the generations. The standardization of letterforms and the development of more robust book design, with chapter headings and page numbers, helped the audience for printed information come to grips with the new information glut.

We are now in the midst of a similar technological flux. There are so many possible visual solutions to the problem of designing information, and so many interaction protocols that the designer and the reader cannot always get it together. If designers are free to develop self-configuring and organic information structures, then readers will need to learn how to read and control them. If this problem is solved, it will pave the way to a new era in information design.

EQUALITY WAY

I BELIEVE THE DECLARATION
THAT "ALL MEN ARE CREATED
EQUAL" IS THE GREAT
FUNDAMENTAL PRINCIPLE
UPON WHICH OUR FREE
INSTITUTIONS REST.

— Abraham Lincoln
1809–1865

Martin Wattenberg

www.bewitched.com

THE ART OF VISUALIZATION

Martin Wattenberg is a digital artist and information designer who originally trained in mathematics. His work for smartmoney.com was the first real-time visualization of the stock market that could be understood by anybody (even me). He is currently based in the Boston area.

The process of information visualization demands a partnership between artist and data. The artist sets in motion the visualization, which, in turn, reveals truths the artist could not have known. The digital metamorphosis of the procedure gives us a new and seemingly limitless palette, where everything is data and any display seems possible.

Revelatory data visualization long predates computers. In the eighteenth century, physicist Ernst Chladni created beautiful images with simple tools. He found that if he sprinkled sand on a metal plate and played music, the sand arranged itself into sinuous rune-like shapes. These mysterious patterns were acclaimed for their elegant symmetry; as data visualization, they let scientists glimpse an invisible world of vibrations, and led the way toward the modern theory of elasticity.

The confluence of beauty and revelation remains the goal today. The design process, though, has been completely transformed. Chladni's data visualizations reflected their subject matter physically and logically. The designer's expressive freedom was limited by the laws of physics, while the data spoke freely.

As digital artists, we have a historic opportunity to make any effect we wish, free from physical constraints. We can take enormous data sets and present them in a spectacular array of ways. They can be space-filling, three-dimensional, hyperbolic, zoomed in or out of or drilled into. But, they can also fail in a variety of ways: by being cluttered, obscure, labyrinthine, or dizzying. A technique that works for a small data set may fall apart as you scale it up. Consider a Venn Diagram (below), a plain-as-day view of three intersecting sets. Moving up to five sets, I ran into unexpected problems—the laws of geometry forced me to draw ovals, not circles. Also, with so many curves, the eye can no longer easily identify the different regions. The clarity has vanished; it is not the information but the visualization technique that speaks most loudly.

As a designer, I take comfort in the thought that while hidden pitfalls await, so do hidden treasures. I have made many attempts to visualize musical form, often involving complex statistical analysis. The only satisfying result was a program that simply drew a musical score as a timeline, connecting repeated passages with translucent arcs. Operating with this single rule, each piece of music—from Bach to Britney Spears—gave rise to a unique form, revealing patterns I never anticipated (opposite). The simplicity of the method allowed room for the data to say something I could not have said myself.

Chladni's brilliant visualization of music depended on physical chance, the happenstance of sand seen dancing on metal. By removing that dependence on chance, computers have given us vast new power, altering the balance between designer and data. Our challenge is to learn how to exercise this power simply and quietly, allowing data the freedom it needs to surprise us.

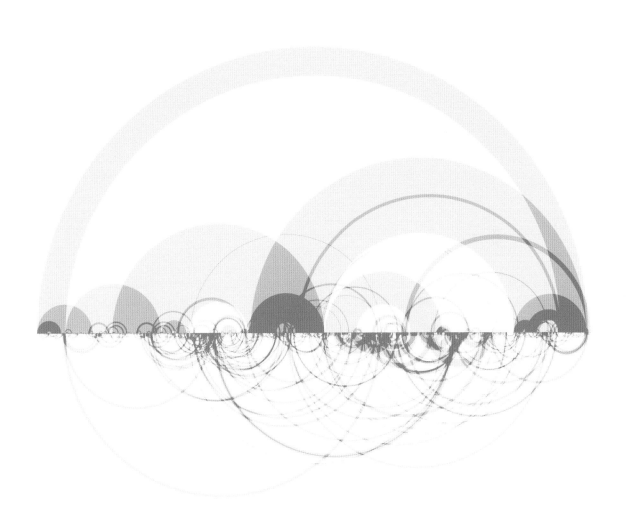

4. Type

When I first heard the word "typography" uttered in the most serious of tones by a designer acquaintance of mine, I let out an insensitive giggle. I thought that only the most self-absorbed person could take something as simple as our system of ABC and proclaim that a kind of grand scientific experiment was in the making. That was until I found myself correcting people who frivolously threw around the word "font," suggesting "typeface" as the more appropriate word to show one's respect. Respect to whom? Not to the typographer, but to the typeface. After all, typefaces have feelings too.

I know from personal experience that type is much more meaningful than any kind of graphic mark we leave on the page. In general, people are uncomfortable with an abstract form because a concrete reaction is difficult to synthesize. Something that is representational or non-abstract, like a depiction of something we can identify, creates an immediate sense of ease. Yet, this feeling of understanding can dissolve when you notice discrepancies between reality and that which is depicted. So, the abstract form that may have confounded you initially starts looking better and better.

Type sits somewhere between the two planes of abstraction and representation, as a kind of conduit between the unreal and real. The marking of three lines—two supported against each other at the top, with a horizontal bar that is anchored to the midpoint of the two lines: an uppercase "A"—is realized with a kind of structural innocence that can be appreciated for a short moment. This simple appreciation morphs into something of greater depth when more letters are added and the formation of coherent words and understandable sentences begins to coalesce. When typography bridges the gap between the raw visual impressions that a single letter can impose upon a viewer and the deepest intention of significance, meaning is born.

I was never truly happy in 1994 when my work took a typographic turn from the purely abstract experimental reactive graphics that had been my initial focus. I had observed that people responded better to my work when they glimpsed something they understood rather than being bathed in a visual abstraction of changing patterns or colored light. At the time, the amusement I perceived in people's eyes as a reaction to my abstract work was far from my artistic intentions; perhaps my typographic turn was driven by my youthful desire to be better known and respected. Pressures on the developing artist are real, and if the artist succumbs, the results are short-lived compromises between that which the world needs and that which the artist can deliver. This is the natural cycle of survival for any individual who wishes to be truly free.

Computers are graduating from 32-bit architectures to 64- and 128-bit native processing capabilities. Where will these advances take digital typography? What comes to my mind immediately is the little error box that pops up in Adobe Illustrator when you try to set the size of type to something really big (just for kicks), and you are politely told that the limit is 1296 points. That distance translates to about a foot and a half, or roughly half a meter. You can trick Illustrator into drawing bigger type by embedding an external illustration file and scaling that file, but even that technique will backfire if you get too aggressive. The promised land of WYSIWYG (What You See Is What You Get) segues into the territories of the NA (Not Allowed). After all, numbers, just like typefaces, have feelings and do not like to be pushed too far. One-hundred-and-twenty-eight-bit numerics will remove all commonly held restrictions, and specifying type the size of a football field ne a letter "A" at the size of the great Sea of Rains on the moon (420 miles or 676 kilometers in diameter). And, when we manage to print it out on the galaxy-class printers of the future, someone with common sense will realize that we could have imagined it all along without any bits at all, by just using our brains.

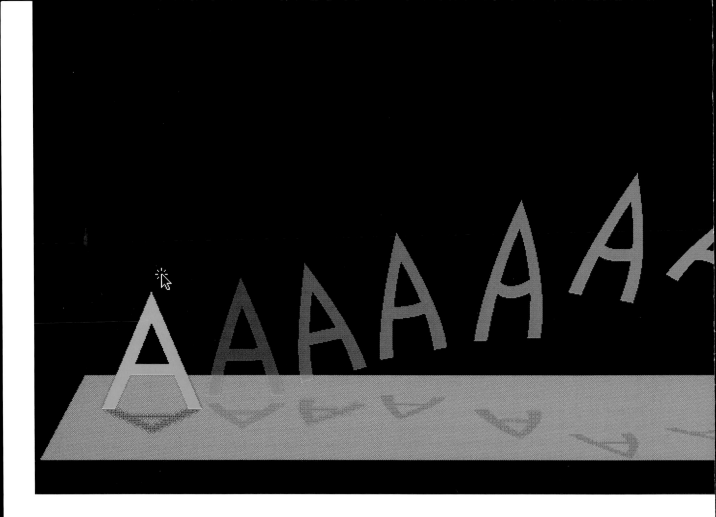

Typography as an area of exploration
culminated with great visual pioneers
like Emil Ruder and Wolfgang Weingart.
However, it never hurts to take a tour through
a beautiful countryside, even if it has been
over-traveled. When inquisitive students are
involved, there is always an opportunity to
find a stone that has been left unturned.

In my mind, typographic work at MIT began
and ended with Peter Cho. A soft-spoken
mechanical-engineering student, Cho phoned
me just a few weeks after my arrival at MIT.
Within minutes, he had expressed a passion for
typography that would have seemed natural
in an art or design school, but certainly out of
place at the Institute. I agreed to take him on,
not knowing the kind of potential he would
eventually show.

FLOATING AND FLUTTERING "A"

Peter Cho, 1996

A few weeks after picking up a computer-graphics manual for the first time in his life, Cho had created an interactive letterform. Like all roman alphabets, he began with the letter "A." This "A" was unlike anything I had ever seen — to describe it in a single word, I would have to say it was definitely "fluttery."

With sufficient coercion from the mouse and thanks to a most intuitive relationship between live motion and letterform, the "A" floats above a plane and gently sways across the screen as if being carefully tugged. Reed Kram was instrumental in guiding Cho to this point, but Cho's subsequent work exceeded everyone's expectations, except for his own.

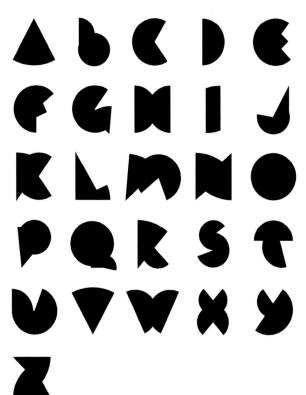

TYPEFACE COMPOSED OF PIE SEGMENTS
Peter Cho, 1997

To create a typeface that is easily malleable in the computational medium, the constituent shapes must be reduced to compact numerical forms. In a course on digital typography, Cho consistently demonstrated a unique skill for marrying extremely simple numerical form with true elegance in craft. This entire uppercase alphabet is derived from twenty-six groups of only ten numbers, and each letter is composed of only two computer-graphic arc primitives.

```
int[][] alphabet = {
          // x1 y1 r1 s1 e1 x2 y2 r2 s2 e2
          {150, 0, 300, 242, 56, 150, 0, 300, 242, 56},              //A
          {60, 103, 105, -90, 180, 160, 200, 105, 180, 360},         //B
          {165, 150, 150, 60, 245, 165, 150, 150, 60, 245},          //C
          {80, 150, 148, -90, 180, 80, 150, 148, -90, 180},          //D
          {165, 150, 150, 53, 260, 250, 145, 90, 135, 90},           //E
          {165, 150, 150, 40, 230, 235, 170, 90, 115, 90},           //F
          {165, 150, 150, 55, 245, 260, 310, 178, 85, 50},           //G
          {30, 150, 150, -90, 180, 270, 150, 150, 90, 180},          //H
          {200, 285, 285, 90, 20, 102, 15, 286, -90, 20},            //I
          {255, -5, 235, -90, -28, 150, 198, 110, 20, -210},         //J
          {30, 310, 310, 55, 35, 180, 150, 150, 55, 250},            //K
          {35, -10, 310, -90, 30, 35, 300, 230, 0, 25},              //L
          {-30, 306, 300, 85, -42, 190, 160, 150, 220, -290},        //M
          {35, 300, 300, 90, -50, 275, 0, 300, -90, -50},            //N
          {150, 150, 150, 0, 360, 150, 150, 150, 0, 360},            //O
          {150, 110, 110, 170, -300, 65, 305, 260, 50, 46},          //P
          {145, 150, 143, -90, 360, 220, 303, 85, 180, -192},        //Q
          {50, 310, 310, 50, 40, 185, 200, 107, 133, 180},           //R
          {153, 95, 95, -90, -233, 150, 190, 110, 90, -250},         //S
          {150, 130, 130, 180, -180, 205, 170, 130, 105, 180},       //T
          {150, 150, 150, 180, 250, 0, 150, 140, 0, 90},             //U
          {150, 300, 300, -242, -56, 150, 300, 300, -242, -56},      //V
          {35, 160, 145, -65, 180, 265, 160, 145, 65, 180},          //W
          {150, 80, 95, 50, -280, 150, 220, 105, 230, -280},         //X
          {140, 90, 100, 125, 180, 120, 140, 160, 55, -180},         //Y
          {30, 20, 250, 0, -45, 290, 290, 260, 180, -60}};           //Z
```

In this later work, Cho addressed a similar problem of expressing the letters of the alphabet using minimal forms, this time with no more than seven rectangular solids per letter. Note the intentional skewed placement of the blocks within each letter to enhance the three-dimensionality of each form.

THREE-DIMENSIONAL TYPEFACE
Peter Cho, 1998

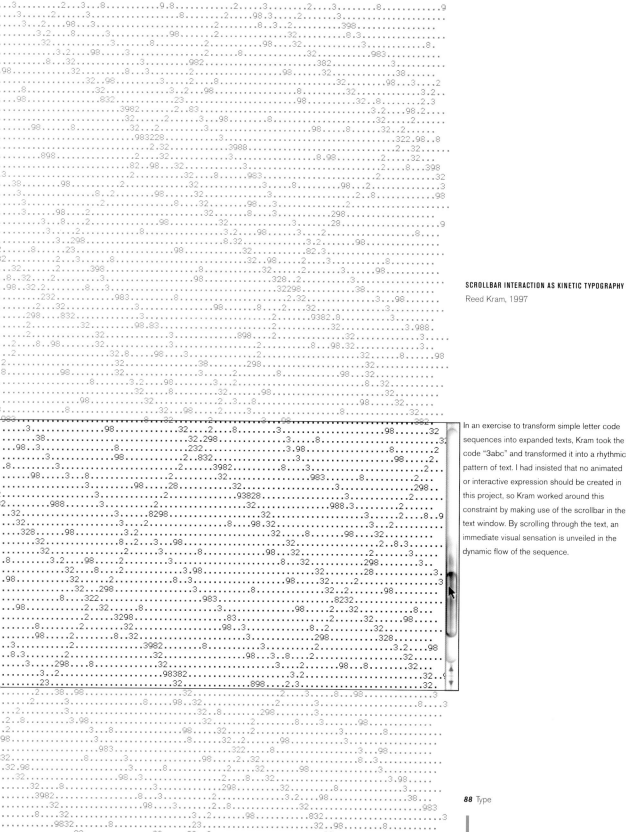

In an exercise to transform simple letter code sequences into expanded texts, Kram took the code "3abc" and transformed it into a rhythmic pattern of text. I had insisted that no animated or interactive expression should be created in this project, so Kram worked around this constraint by making use of the scrollbar in the text window. By scrolling through the text, an immediate visual sensation is unveiled in the dynamic flow of the sequence.

HUMAN GENOME DATA VISUALIZED
Benjamin Fry, 2001

A generation of students after Kram, Fry created a texture made of type. In this case, the large quantity of type has a reason – to represent the genetic sequence of a chromosome in the human genome as a tiny alphabet of ACGT's that stand for the amino acids comprising DNA: Adenine, Cytosine, Guanine, and Thymine.

In a course on digital typography, I asked students to create text-based analogs to the visual-based filters commonly found in programs like PhotoShop. If blurring an image in PhotoShop creates a softer image, what kind of implications are there for blurring text?

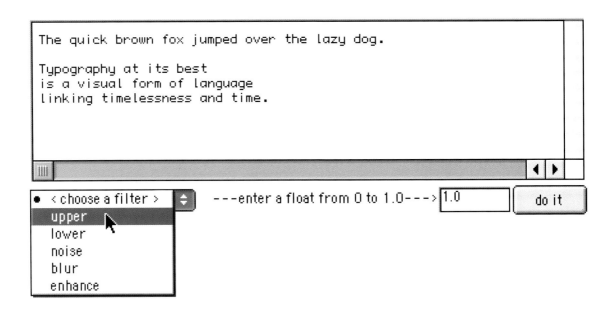

THE QUICK BROWN FOX JUMPED OVER THE LAZY DOG.

TYPOGRAPHY AT ITS BEST
IS A VISUAL FORM OF LANGUAGE
LINKING TIMELESSNESS AND TIME.

The most commonly used text filter is the command to change every letter to uppercase.

the quick brown fox jumped over the lazy dog.

typography at its best
is a visual form of language
linking timelessness and time.

Converting text to all lowercase letters is also possible, but not as popular.

ENHANCE, NOISE AND BLUR FILTERS FOR TEXT

Peter Cho, 1997

```
((       ( (      (        (      (( (   (
The quick brown fox jumped over the lazy dog.
    )         ) )                   )   )

(       (  ( ( ( (
Typography at its best
 )) ) ) )
            ( (      ( (
is a visual form of language
                    )  )
(   (    (   (           (  (
linking timelessness and time.
    )
```

```
The ghuiccck pirowhn hogs chuemfed oher the laksi doj.

Tefojraprhe at its plest
is a beisual pormn oh lankuaje
linkinj tiemelessness and tieme.
```

The enhance filter accentuates ascenders with a
parenthesis placed above each instance, and
descenders with a parenthesis below each example.

The noise filter adds letters that interfere with
the original spellings.

```
The quick brown fox juTmhpee dq uoivcekr  btrhoew nl afzoy  djougm.ped over the lazy dog.

TypographTyy proegmraaiprihsy  remains
a source of tar useo udrecle; gohft ,t rue delight.
true knowledge,t r tureu ek nsouwrlperdigsee,. true surprise.
```

Taking each line of text, the blur filter overlays
a copy of itself onto the line, resulting in a
collision of letters that at first appears
haphazard but on closer inspection reveals
the process.

```
Zee qooeeck broon fux joomped oofer zee lazy dug.

Typugraphu at its best
is a feesooal furm ooff lungooage
leenkeeng teemelessness und teeme.
```

```
Tha bnick qromu fox jnwdap ovar tha lesy po6.

Tydobredhy rameruz
e zonrra of trna pali6ht,
trna kuomlap6a, trna znrdriza.
```

LINGUISTIC BLURRING FILTER

Tom White, 1997

PURE TEXT-BASED INVERSION FILTER

Chloe Chao, 1997

Another example of a blur filter, this method
uses a faux-linguistic technique to produce
texts that carry a fake foreign accent. Here,
White chooses Swedish, which to him sounds
like a blur.

Chao interprets blur as an inversion of the
text by substituting invertible letter pairs or
numbers, for example, "b" for "q," "g" for "6,"
and "d" for "p."

White transforms the physical simulation of a bouncing ball into an ad-hoc type design. A physicist understands a bouncing object by its gravity, its initial position in space and how bouncy it is when it hits the ground. By changing the parameters of these three criteria White creates a letterform from the path traced by the ball as it travels forward in space and time. Only nine parameters encode the shape of each element of type.

Although I recall an expression of disgust from a set of elite Japanese designers when they saw White's construction, the typeface is more legible than you might think. Granted, the aesthetic principles of this alphabet may not follow any Platonic rules of beauty, yet it is still possible to appreciate the rawness of the marks and White's clear and admirable lack of fear in visualizing the hitherto unseen.

Control Center

Initial x	0.1	
Initial y	0.82	
Initial dx	0.06	
Initial dy	−0.13	
Gravity	1.27	
Elasticity	0.89	
X Spin	0.96	
# of Frames	143.0	
BallSize	0.2	

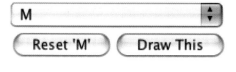

M

Reset 'M'   Draw This

ROBOTIC ARM AS TYPEFACE
Nikita Pashenkov, 2001

Pashenkov turned a brief obsession with industrial manufacturing robots into a slow-moving ballet of rigid jointed forms that posed as letters of the alphabet. This "alphabot" does not have an actual function, nor does it express an emotion. By silently morphing into any character of the alphabet on demand, the alphabot quietly represents the true workhorse of communication—typography.

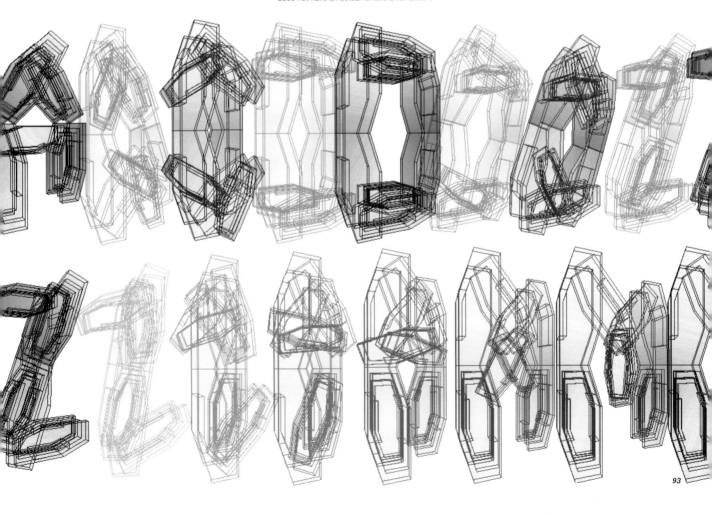

A modern interpretation of ancient hieroglyphics, the symbols here represent sounds. In this phonetic alphabet, White's animated letterforms emulate the passage of air along the throat, over the tongue, past the teeth, and through the lips to form the sound of each letter or phoneme.

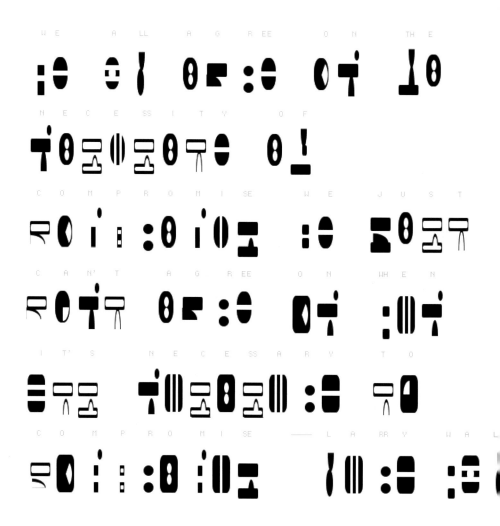

Representation of the word "of": *Air is ejected through the throat for the "o,"* *stopped by the teeth and lips to create the "f,"* *and released to complete the word.*

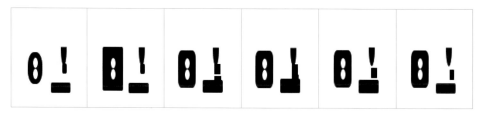

TYPEFACE VISIBLE ONLY WHEN IN MOTION
Bradley Geilfuss, 1997

In response to an exercise in producing a typeface that is inherently in motion, Geilfuss created a typeface that is only legible when animated. The lines' exact density and range of motion are adjusted using the mouse, and the constituent patterns reveal moments of legibility.

With a charming repertoire of good-natured
American Pop artifacts, Pashenkov created
this piece shortly after arriving at MIT. Lying
somewhere between a tool for 3-D construction
and a music sequencer, the work is a variety
of mini experiences of iconic delight and
interaction.

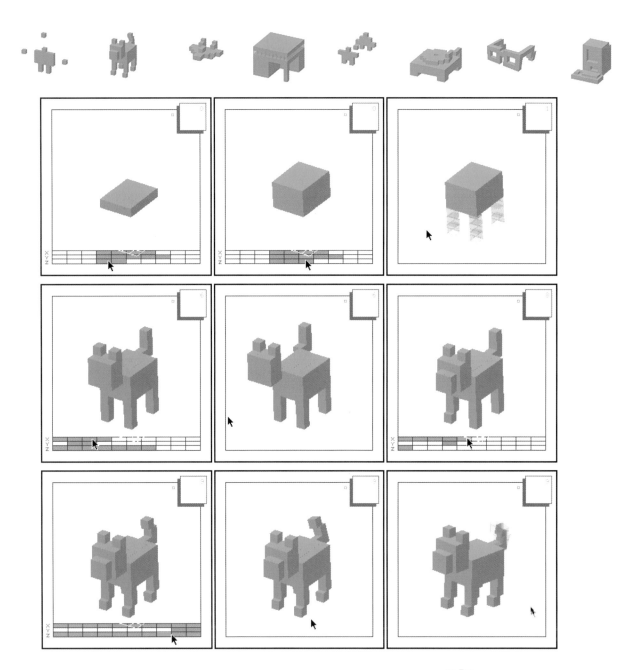

Today,

the dog ran away. / ran out to lunch.

I went to the store to kill the clerk. / to buy laundry detergent. / buy olives. / tomatoes. / ice cream.

I went to San Fransisco to visit some friends.

to the park and played ball. / and got mugged! / read a nice book. / relaxed.

Mother's and took her out to lunch. / and helped her bake cookies.

TYPING DIRECTLY INTO A TREE STRUCTURE
Joshua Nimoy, 1999

I invited Joshua Nimoy to MIT one summer when he was still an undergraduate at UCLA. After a simple bit of direction on how to realize a way of fracturing texts into a treelike form, Nimoy nimbly created this system for producing texts that branch off in various directions mid-sentence.

When directing experiments, I often discover how quickly a simple idea I have follows one of two paths in a student's brain. The first is the literal translation of the idea, which in actuality is uninteresting and the idea remains mine. The second and more interesting path follows the idea as it grows into something many times greater than I could ever imagine, and truly belongs to the student.

Peter Cho

At times, work can be driven by simple circumstance or logic. In this case, I had complained to my students that our 3-D tracking hardware was sorely underused and a wasted resource. Cho responded with this two-handed typing system that fluidly composes words from a series of gestures. Each motion is linked to a particular letter of the alphabet; for example, an upward motion triggers an "A," while a downward motion results in a "Z."

Mathematics can often be an overbearing
theme in the computational artistic realm.
This is no accident, of course, because the
computer is the purest form of math. But,
having witnessed infinite variations of
subjectively colorized Mandelbrot sets that
have been declared "art," one must wonder
where the art begins and the math exits. Cho
ties a commonly used computational geometry
algorithm for partitioning space, called the
Voronoi Diagram, to a light implantation of type,
subtly nesting message within math.

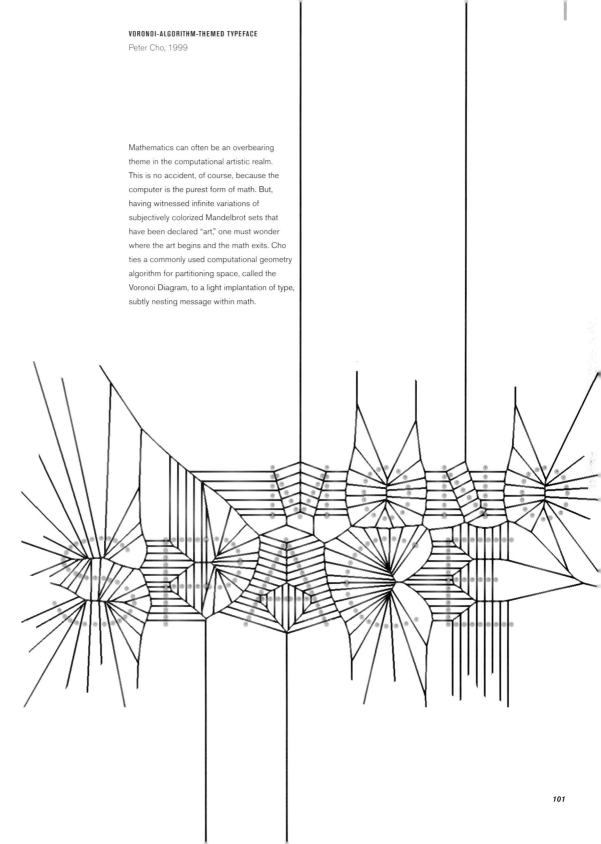

WEBCRAWLER AS SYSTEM OF TYPE TORNADOS
Benjamin Fry, 2001

Fry released a writhing typographic creature that grows as it traverses the web hungry for new information to assimilate into its form.

Websites are swept into swirling tornados that embody the chaos of information on the web.

Synonyms are connected in chains and orthogonal meanings are spawned as new graphs in this confused swell of information that ponders the meaning of a single word. The information grows from this single word and comprehensively follows a train of semantically similar words: anger, acrimony, animosity, annoyance, the chain can go on forever.

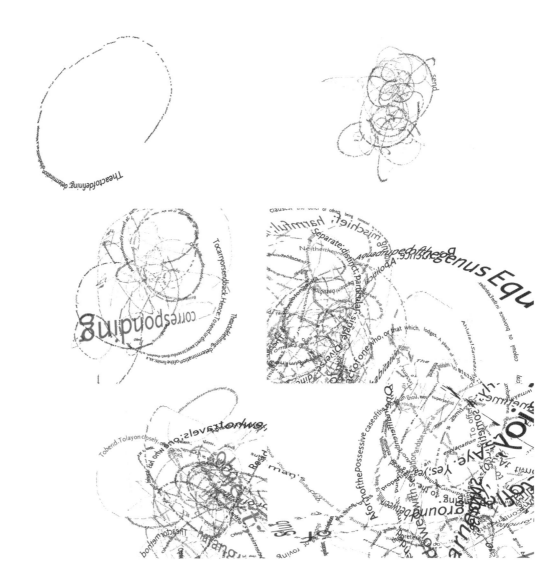

MESSAGE COMPOSED WITH HANDMADE KINETIC TYPE
Peter Cho, 1998

In response to an email critique I sent to Cho
regarding his 3-D typography work, he set an old
man straight with this animation that uses one
of his custom-made typographic systems and the
text of my message.

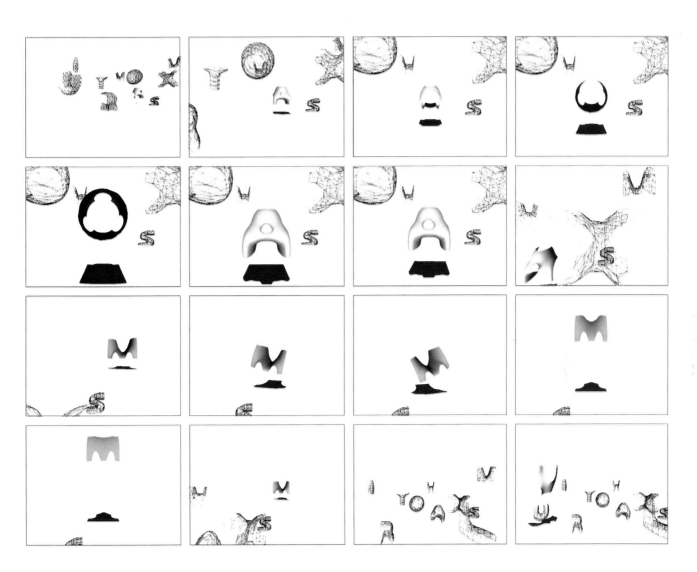

With a dynamic menagerie of playful animals from "A" to "Z," Cho demonstrates the expressive use of blobby 3-D forms with only minimal mathematic flavoring.

ALPHABET ZOO
Peter Cho, 1998

The standard final assignment I used to set my class was to transmute a stream of data communication. The communication stream in question was the server, which used to pass messages from any connected client to all connected clients simultaneously, in the way that Internet-based chat systems work. I stopped setting this assignment because of the technical difficulties of keeping the server running reliably. To illustrate the point, I spent half a day just getting these old applets running.

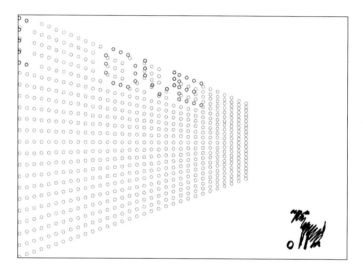

5: I moved to (0.36,0.65) I moved to (0.36,0.4) I moved to (0.35,0

DOG WATCHING THE MESSAGE BOARD
Bradley Geilfuss, 1997

CHATTING WITH A CIRCULAR THEME
Peter Cho, 1997

Opting for the passive approach, Geilfuss simply takes all the messages received on the channel and places them on his signboard. The dog wags his tail whilst waiting for new messages. When messages cease to appear, the dog goes to sleep, and his happy, puppy-oriented dreams appear on the signboard.

Taking the unifying element of a circle, Cho's arc-based alphabet gracefully knits together the appearance and disappearance of circular forms as messages that silently engage the communicator. Here, I type "hello," and the message swiftly unfolds from a circular form.

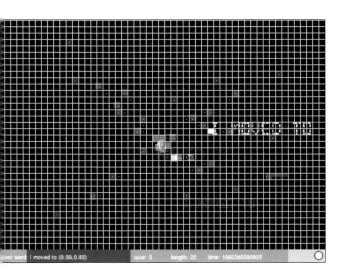

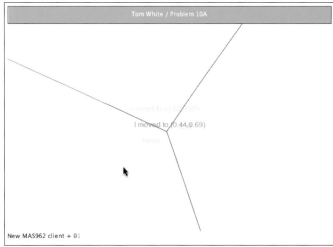

TALKING IN A BATTLEFIELD

Matthew Grenby, 1997

SOCIAL MAP COMPOSED IN REAL TIME

Tom White, 1997

Grenby creates an elaborate grid of all the messages waiting in the system, thereby tracking the flow of communication between clients. The set up of a grid and sparsely colored blocks moving autonomously brings to mind old video games of battles.

Instead of typing, you broadcast the position of your mouse with a click that sends out the text, "I moved to (x, y)." As clients begin to use the server, a Voronoi Diagram maps the emergent structure of interconnected communications across parties.

Peter Cho

www.pcho.net

DYNAMIC TYPOGRAPHY: PAST, PRESENT, AND FUTURE

Peter Cho graduated from MIT in 1999, and left for Los Angeles to pursue his dream of creating film titles at Imaginary Forces. Today, he resides in LA, refining his craft on the UCLA graduate program.

Many people read more text on a computer, television, PDA, or cell phone than they do on paper. How did this happen? Over the last few decades, our relationship with technology has developed to the point where watching, viewing, and reading the graphic displays that surround us seems a natural part of our lives. On-screen type, digital by nature, is undoubtedly cheaper to publish and distribute than its analog counterpart. Dynamic typography, or type that moves, offers some unique opportunities over the static typography on a page. As a time-based medium, dynamic typography allows for a cinematic approach, an approach with voices and characters, with pace, suspense, surprise, and storytelling. Interactivity can also be combined with moving typography to navigate a non-linear narrative or to convey a complex information space.

Dynamic typography's history began with the illusion of motion on the static page and went on to include flip books, film, television, and the computer screen. When considering animated typography, it is useful to look at static typography in which the placement or design of the text gives added meaning to the words. In the late 1910s, the Dada and Futurist movements looked at how the positioning of words and letters could enhance or change the poetic meaning. Concrete poets of the 1950s and 1960s took these experiments further, developing visual poems intended to be viewed like paintings. Graphic designers and artists, such as László Moholy-Nagy and Robert Massin, used the page as a medium for expressive and dimensional typography. Typography that actually moves originated with the temporal

medium of film. Title-sequence design emerged as an artform in itself in the 1950s with Saul Bass's elegant films-within-films; it then resurfaced in the mid-1990s with the work of Kyle Cooper, among others. Current-day software tools, such as After Effects and Flash, make it easy to create a text animation. So, what desktop publishing did for print (making it possible for anyone with a computer to produce professional-looking printed work) these software tools may do for dynamic typography (making it possible for anyone with the software to create broadcast-quality motion graphics).

Regardless of the historical precedents for dynamic typography, today it is most commonly seen in advertising. Animated text messages abound on television and the web, mostly because someone is trying to grab our attention to sell us something. Some information graphics have also broken through, however: In recent years, a news "crawl" has taken over a chunk of the screen space on most news, sports, music, and entertainment cable networks. Television advertisers have realized that the animated written word, sometimes in concert with the spoken word, can capture eyeballs, while saving the ad agency from a costly live-action film shoot. Advertising messaging has become more important to corporations as they vie for our attention and try to establish brand recognition in the twenty-first century. This pervasiveness is bound to reach into our "real lives" as advertisers go beyond the screen and into the physical spaces around us. Dealing with this escalating media saturation will be a challenge in the near future.

While the digital revolution has meant that our attention spans have become shorter due to the growing barrage of dynamic text, computation and digital technology can be combined with typography to explore something expressive and beautiful. Recent technological advances have introduced email, cell-phone text messaging, instant messaging online, and blogs—all new textual forms with their own structures and rules. We may soon see a thus far unimagined written form using dynamic type in an innovative way, a form that may bridge the gap between the spoken and written word, much as real-time messaging has begun to do. We may see the introduction of an intelligent font that can hear you or speak to you and that can demonstrate tone and inflection in a beautiful way. This font's characters may have a higher level of knowledge about their shapes and may change or exaggerate their features—while keeping the integrity of the form intact—to convey the emotional context of a message. Another future direction may involve the manipulation of the structure of written text, using hypertext or other user interaction, to add depth to traditional linear storytelling. If this is the future, then dynamic typography will be capable of making text come alive in elegant and inventive ways. I eagerly await that day.

Yugo Nakamura

www.yugop.com

THE INTERNET TREE

Yugo Nakamura is a digital artist and designer who lives in Tokyo. He is the pre-eminent design force within the Flash medium, and I think he will hold this position of leadership for many years to come.

A tree is made from the connection of leaves and branches, but a tree is not merely the sum of its branches and leaves. A "tree" yields a new dimension of recognition: It grows, it goes through different phases, and it dies. From the perspective of a single leaf, however, the image of the tree as a whole cannot be grasped. Certainly, "leaf" and "tree" are physically connected, but there is a discontinuity in recognition: Each exists in its own dimensionally distinct space.

I investigate the potential of Internet-based interactive design. In the design of interactions that operate within the client-server model are various aspects that are unique to the Internet and for which the tree metaphor is useful. In the Internet, the space of the "leaf" influences the space of the "tree." The space of the leaf, i.e., a single computer, is a closed space in which logical order explicitly operates. Conversely, the space of the tree, i.e., the Internet, is vague and broad—a world in which mass psychology and the sciences of probability and statistics are complexly intertwined. These two spaces are physically connected, but their working methods exist in two different states that are exact opposites of each other.

I am considering two approaches to interaction design that will intersect these two states. The first is a composition of differences in method, such as simple versus complex, precise versus vague. For example, a simple expression is released into the chaos of Internet space. The expression acquires life and begins to function independently; metamorphosis becomes a function of feedback. Within the synergistic movement of the expression and its surrounding environment, there is a vivid beauty. In the vocabulary of the composition that yields this dynamic movement, I believe that there are many variations and opportunities.

The other approach is more practical, using a community rather than method as the primary unit. The Internet is not just the closed space of a single person's transaction and interaction. It is a large unspecified group, and insight on interaction at an even larger dimension is critical. Rather than consider the entire Internet, which is basically of unknown dimension, it is more effective to study "communities," which are tangible units. My own lifestyle is based on the premise of various communities. In which aspect of the community does the expression work, and in what way does it generally work? By repeating the actions and reactions through trial and error, I believe that we get closer to the domain in which the community and the "live" direct expression can become one.

From the standpoint of the leaf, you may not be able to entirely grasp the image of the tree, but with a little imagination you can work toward a greater sphere of understanding. Repeating this trial and error, somehow the form of the tree might change just a little. With this in mind, I continue to design.

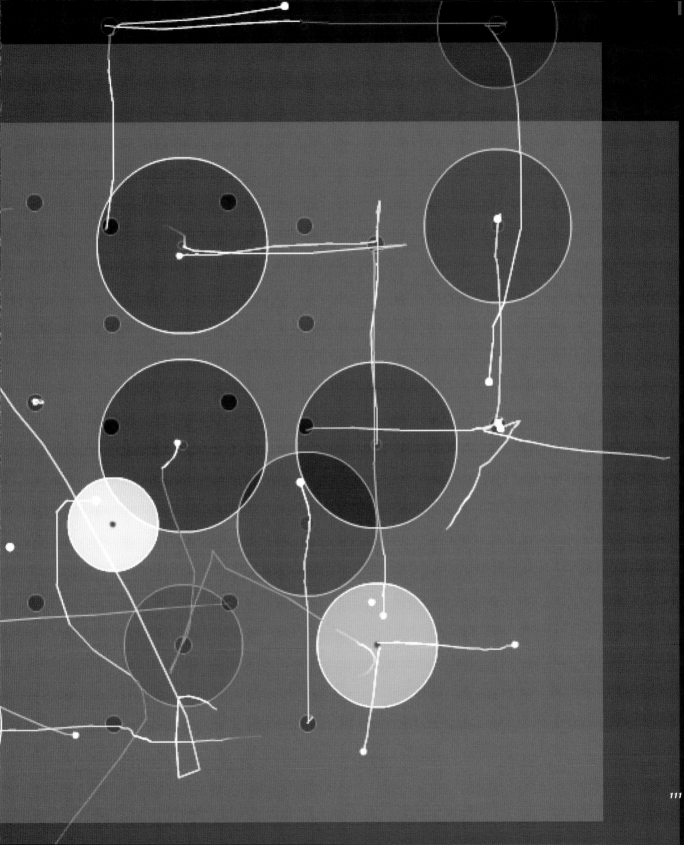

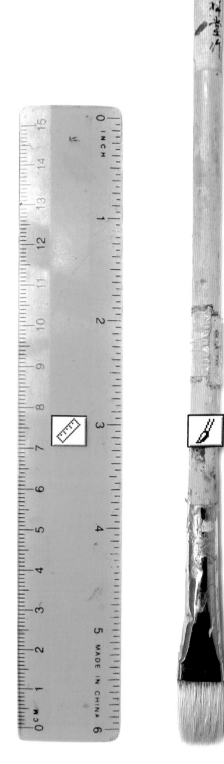
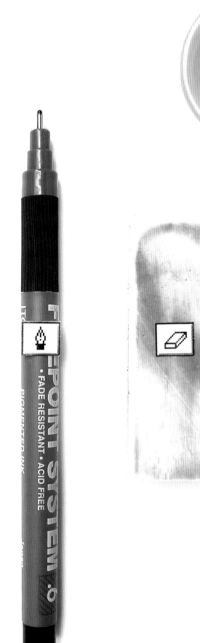

5. Tool

I expended much effort in my early career trying to negate the conventional belief, borne in the 1980s, that the computer was nothing more than a new kind of pencil. "It is not a tool; it is a new material for expression," I found myself self-righteously chanting to unbelieving masses across the globe. Luckily for me, the web turned prophecy into reality. Today, we witness the relentless daily expansion of digital expression across a variety of emerging platforms, such as Flash, SVG, and QuickTime. As all of this was happening, I began to recognize my own limitations as a creative, and decided to focus on developing my career as a professor, with fragments of concrete thought left along the way as small tokens of authorship.

Reflecting on when I got started in this medium, however, I vividly remember a fresher, wilder time that was civilized by one of the true progenitors of digital media arts, Mr. Naomi Enami, who, during the pre-dot.com era, founded a forward-looking electronic media publishing house in Tokyo called Digitalogue. Without a convenient method for previewing and distributing media like the web, Enami was a latter-day Marco Polo in his worldly travels, gathering and trading digital media and creating a new Silk Road. But, unlike most publishers of digital media, Enami was also an avid user of the tools for digital expression. We often debated the virtues of seeing the computer as a tool versus a new material, and consistently concluded that it was indeed an exciting material but an equally useful tool.

Users of tools are much more prevalent than makers of tools. This imbalance has traditionally been rooted in the vast difference in skill levels required for using a tool compared to making a tool: To use a tool on the computer, you need do little more than point and click; to create a tool, you must understand the arcane art of computer programming.

A strange reverse phenomenon is in motion today: As programming becomes easier and more accessible, the tools for expression are becoming more complex and difficult to use. Programming tools are increasingly oriented toward fill-in-the-blank approaches to the construction of code, making it easy to create programs but resulting in software with less originality and fewer differentiating features. The experience of using the latest software, meanwhile, has made even expert users less likely to dispose of their manuals, as the operation of the tools is no longer self-evident. Can we, therefore, envision a future where software tools are coded less creatively? Furthermore, will it someday be the case that tools are so complex that they become an obstacle to free-flowing creativity? I think so. What happens when the Internet grows in speed ten-fold, hundred-fold, and beyond? Does the nature of content naturally improve as a direct result of "more"?

I remember Enami's secret stash of the latest and greatest in digital media hits from around the world—a hodgepodge collection of dirty Zip disks, floppy disks, and CD-ROMs of questionable origin. In the early days, he showed me with great pride his latest finds from France, London, Seoul or more obscure provenances. Yet, as the computer increased in speed and in its ability to handle greater data capacities, Enami's finds, paradoxically, were less frequent. We found ourselves marveling more often at the drastic reduction in size and cost of the computer rather than the emerging talent.

Enami's health took a severe downturn in 1999 when he entered a long coma, and, sadly, he is no longer able to engage with the regular world. If he were still healthy, I imagine he would be awestruck by today's technology, but much less so about the work being done. There is a lot to see, but merely that: a lot.

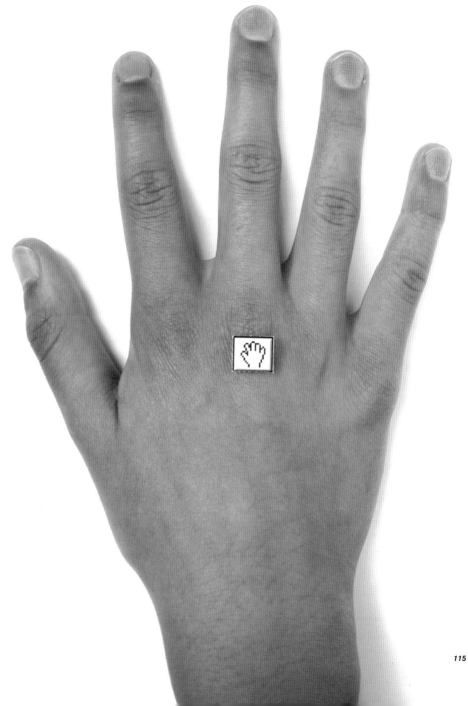

In this section, the conventional notion of a digital "tool" is challenged by a hearty group of students who wish to redefine the norm.

PAINTING IN FREQUENCY SPACE
Golan Levin, 1998

Much of the processing in such image-manipulation programs as PhotoShop occurs in a dimensional space that we cannot see. The frequency representation of an image is the magical gateway to things we take for granted, such as the rapid blurring of an on-screen image. I set an exercise to paint directly into the frequency space of an image, in the spirit of painting on the right brain with a left-brain mentality.

Here, a photograph is loaded into the window on the left, and its frequency representation is computed and displayed on the right. Lower frequencies are in the middle, and higher frequencies appear farther from the center. If you have used an equalizer on a stereo, the concept of frequency space will be a familiar one: Low frequency is the bass, high frequency the treble. Manipulating the frequencies has a direct effect on the imported photo.

Brush selection is made in the lower pane of the window.

Some low- and mid-frequencies are disturbed by the brush.

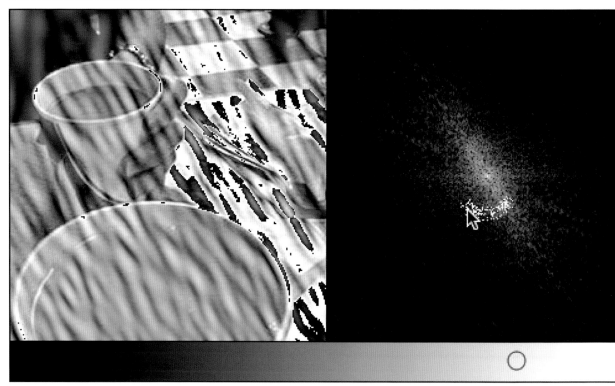

An innocent smear in frequency space results in a global distortion of the image.

Fry reworked the concept of a brush to make it more appropriate to painting in frequency space. The resulting swirl brush evenly paints across a specific band of frequencies by tracing circles around a center point.

Note the irregularly positioned and sized palette of grays to the right of the main interface canvas as opposed to the single band of gray presented in Levin's applet (opposite). The same function is achieved in both examples, but with clearly distinct styles of visual finishes.

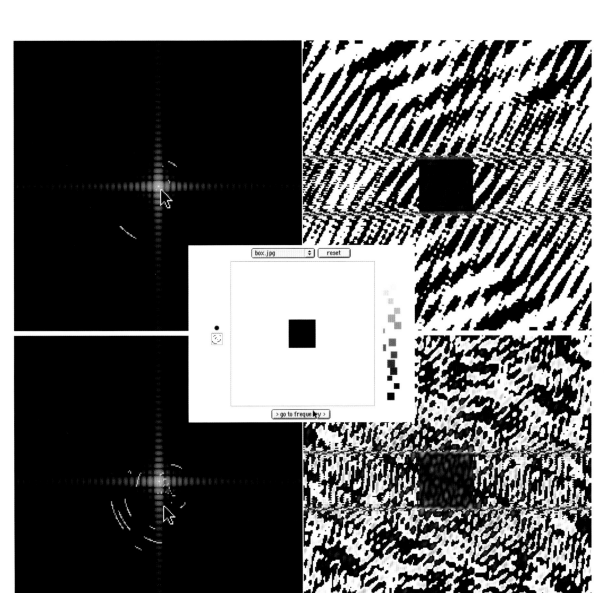

MOVING THE WINDOW INSTEAD OF MOVING THE TOOL
Bradley Geilfuss, 1998

Many visual definitions of a tool with a single functional specification are possible. Here, Geilfuss introduces two static thin red lines as the brush, around which the underlying image repositions itself, reversing the normal relationship of brush to canvas. This interface provides no obvious functional enhancement, but it certainly acts as a conversation point about the assumptions of how digital media should behave under the brush.

MAKE YOUR PAINTBRUSH ANYWHERE YOU WANT
Elise Co, 1998

This exercise revolved around painting only with the colors derived from images that had been digitally photographed by the students. Co created the unexpected in her method of brush selection: Drag anywhere within the light-gray pane on the right and the size of the dragged area becomes the size of the brush—an approach that clearly violates conventional user interface wisdom that says the flat areas of the screen are simply there as non-interactive color fields. However, the user's reaction is not one of horror, rather a natural reminiscence about testing a pencil on scrap paper.

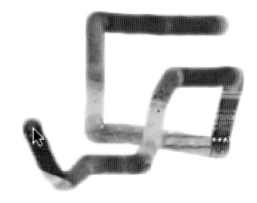

PAINT IN ANY DIRECTION FOR THE UNEXPECTED

Benjamin Fry, 1998

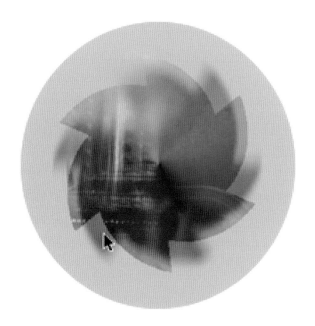

Achieving a similar effect to that created by a pencil with a single multi-colored core, this tool transcends the simple fun of smearing many colors into a logical scheme. Fry created an elaborate six-pointed spinner that controls the relationship between the hue that is painted and the direction of the brush.

 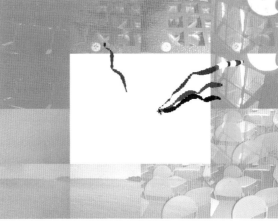

DIP YOUR PAINTBRUSH INTO A PHOTO
Peter Cho, 1998

What if you could dip your paintbrush into a photograph and paint using a palette of colors derived from the surrounding scenery? Cho explores this captivating concept, and also introduces a motion-sensitive brush—big movements result in a thick stroke while smaller ones produce thinner lines.

MIXING A VARIETY OF IMAGES WITH A SWIRL OF THE MOUSE

Benjamin Fry, 1998

When does a tool cease to be a tool and more a work of art? Perhaps when all interaction with the tool results in expressions that are more the signature of the tool than the artist. This does not preclude the possibility that an interactive art piece might prefer a particular person, in much the same way as a painting might look better in a gallery than a kitchen.

To continue the color-painting-tool exercise, I asked students to remove the functions of the tool and create personally meaningful interactions. Fry produced a swirling space that is always dependent upon mouse position. After the initial dizziness subsides, you relish a private dance in which the applet is transformed into an everchanging artwork.

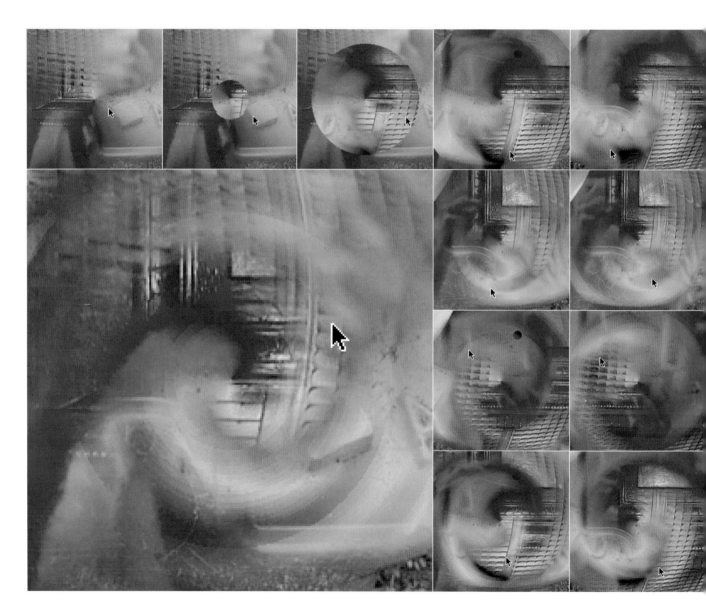

How does one transfer the energy from one photographic event to another? Downie selectively extracts and transfers motion from one image to another. The interface is opaque, but the piece is nonetheless made captivating by the depth of function achieved.

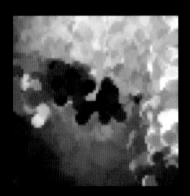
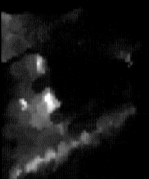

The thin red line (see p. 118) returns in
Geilfuss's motion painting system. On the right,
the vertical cross sections of gulleys on the
image of water are translated as disturbance
patterns and overlaid on the images of the
building on the left. Consequently, the wave
image drives the building into a newly found
watery existence. This simple algorithm can
easily be applied to produce a fiery image
derived from fire or a foggy image derived
from clouds.

(see p. 118)

PLAYBACK OF AN IMAGE ONTO AN IMAGE
Bradley Geilfuss, 1998

SPEED AS A CLOAKING DEVICE
Tom White, 1998

In the art of photography, the relationship between background and foreground often determines an image's success. In an exercise to communicate this delicate balance, White uses temporal expression in a most basic way. A slider at the bottom of the interface is adjusted to select the importance of foreground over background. As background importance is elevated, a rapid succession of small images appears as the foreground. When the background is fully selected, the foreground changes so rapidly that all you really notice is the background; conversely, when the foreground is chosen, the image is still.

foreground   background

oreground   background

Presented with the challenge of amplifying the background of an image, Co produced what she calls "image origami," whereby a freehand stroke around the edge of an image creates a corresponding digital fold. By making the background areas a playground for expression, Co detracts attention from the center of the image.

PAINT PARTICLES THAT TRACE A HAND
Golan Levin, 1998

Here, Levin has created a system of free-
flowing paint bristles with minds of their own.
The only mandate heeded by the bristles'
collective brain is to attend to a rough
photographic map.

Golan Levin

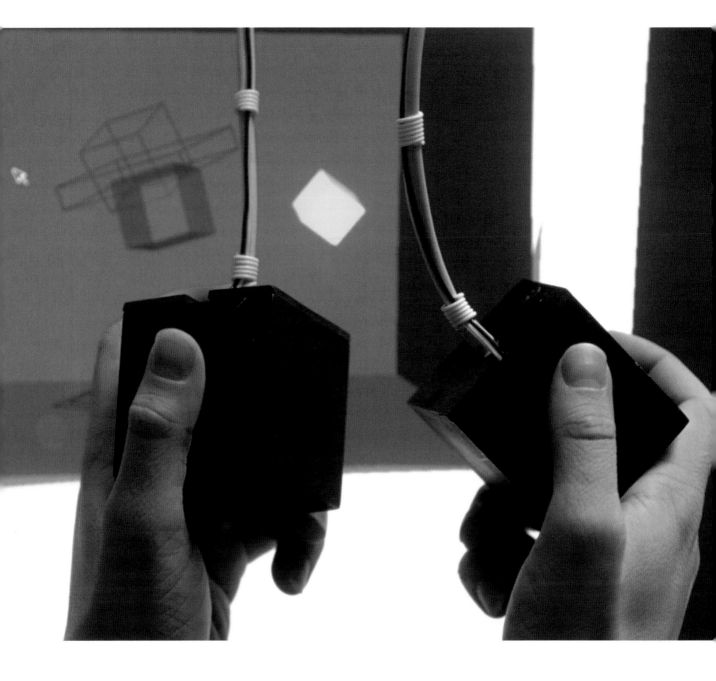

THREE DIMENSIONS TO THREE DIMENSIONS
Reed Kram, 1997

Using an off-the-shelf 3-D-sensing system, Kram experimented with the visual interactions between two cube-shaped marionettes that bounced against each other. Around the same time, we began to investigate live performances as an alternative manifestation of creatively constructed digital tools for expression.

AUDIO/VISUAL PERFORMANCE SYSTEM
Reed Kram, 1998

Kram's thesis work is a modernist interpretation of the music turntable used by deejays. It demonstrates a clear difference between the idea of a tool for everyone and a tool for a professional audience (for example, a musical instrument). Gentle mouse adjustments result in volume and pitch variations in a set of sound samples that are represented as cylinders in an orchestra that only Kram can direct.

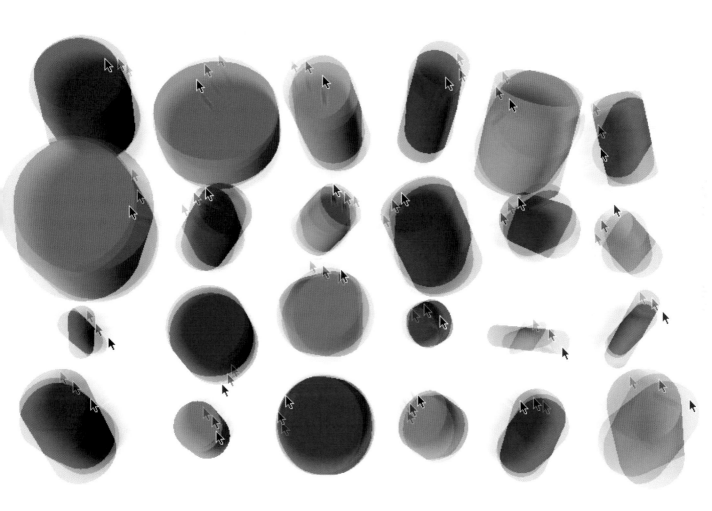

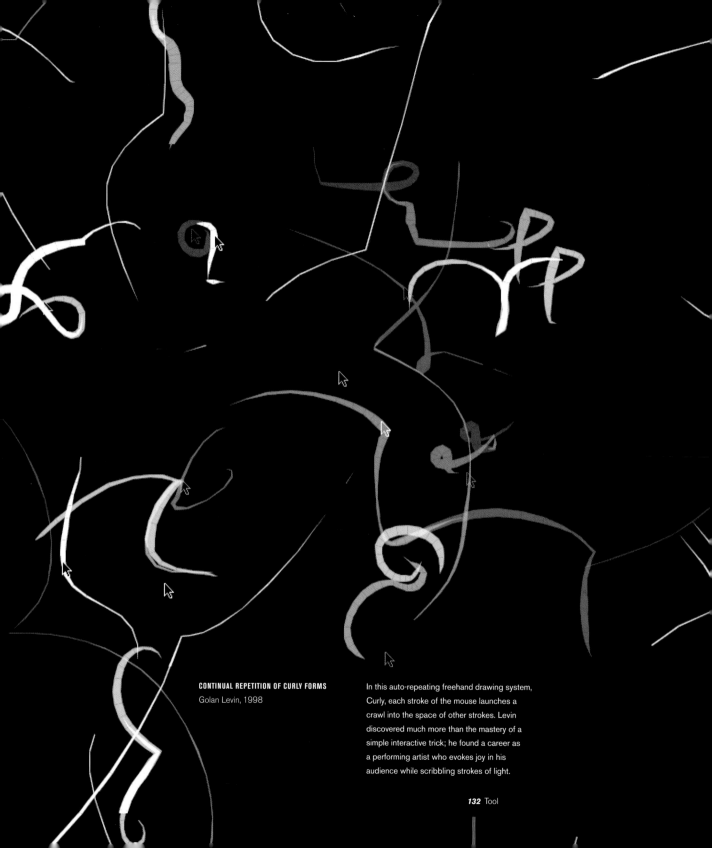

CONTINUAL REPETITION OF CURLY FORMS
Golan Levin, 1998

In this auto-repeating freehand drawing system, Curly, each stroke of the mouse launches a crawl into the space of other strokes. Levin discovered much more than the mastery of a simple interactive trick; he found a career as a performing artist who evokes joy in his audience while scribbling strokes of light.

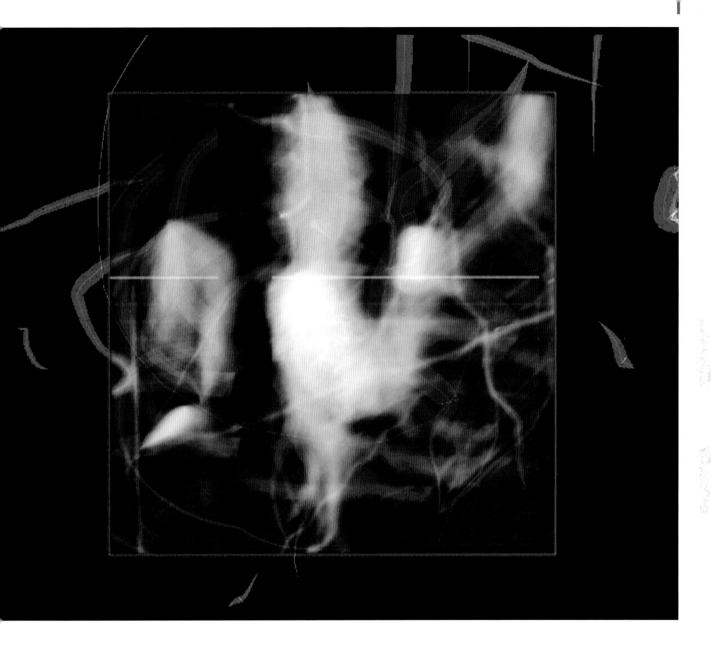

My dissatisfaction with the lack of sound
processing in our group and our subsequent
concentration on this area resulted in sounds
that would eventually make me keep quiet.
Levin reworked Curly to synthesize sounds that
directly related to any freehand mark scribbled
on a dynamic photograph.

PHOTOGRAPH AS PHONOGRAPH
Golan Levin, 1999

OPTICAL DEEJAY SYSTEM
Nikita Pashenkov, 2002

Having hidden his penchant for deejaying for at least a year, Pashenkov converted a conventional turntable into an optical performance system for his thesis project. Perhaps more than any student I have ever worked with, Pashenkov has an uncanny knack for taking budget-basement electronic parts and reinventing them as unique applications.

Here, he reverse engineered an optical barcode reader (that he obtained free of charge), which became the technological centerpiece of the optical turntable.

Optical disks are programmed on the computer as illustrations, which are then printed on a laser printer. A circle is cut with a compass and a hole is

punched in the middle. The paper disk is now spun on the optical turntable. The screen shows a representation of the disk being read in real time.

I discovered Manor as he was graduating in astrophysics from MIT. A year working with David Small had affirmed the nascent artist within him, and he immediately got to work on the computer, producing a variety of systems for his unique brand of live cinematic performance. Incorporating archival footage, sound samples and live video, Manor synthesizes visual experiences that blur past, present, and future with a lot of love.

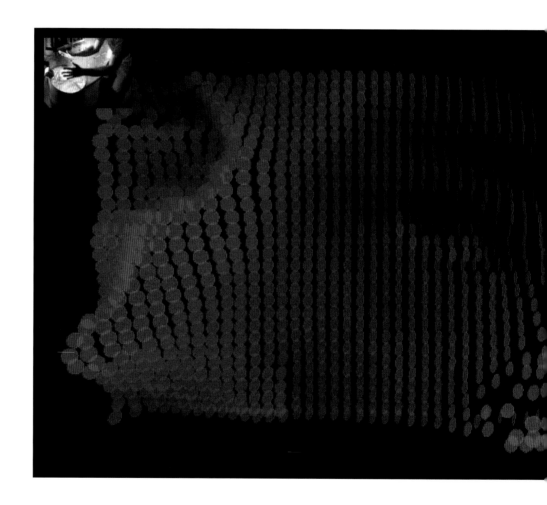

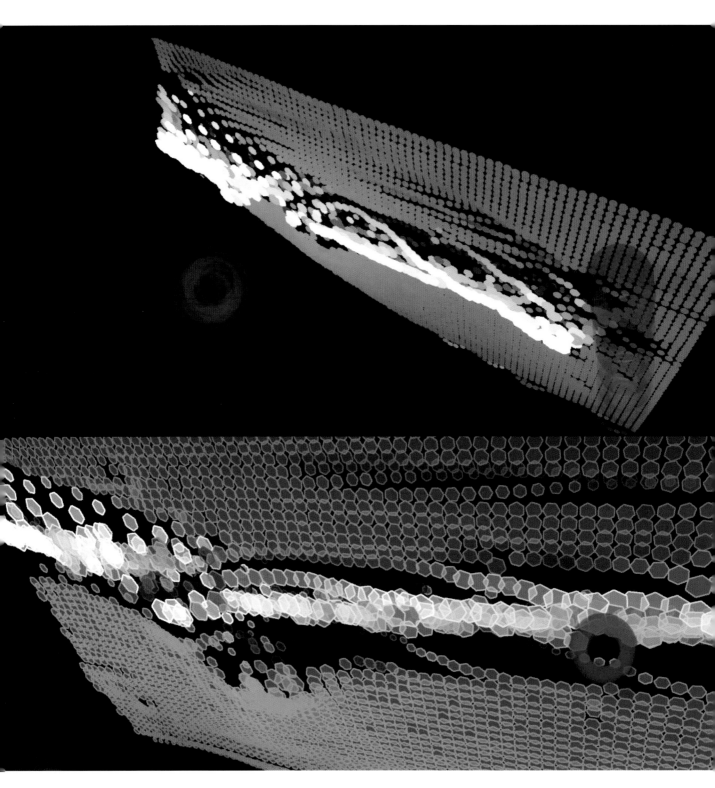

MANIPULABLE CINEMATIC LANDSCAPES
Justin Manor, 2003

When the Steven Spielberg movie *Minority Report* was released, it had a special effect—the ability to browse video with hand gestures—that many perceived as already existing at the Media Lab. This was not true, so Manor fixed the inaccuracy in his thesis project on glove-controlled cinematic landscapes.

Golan Levin

www.flong.com

IS THE COMPUTER A TOOL?

Golan Levin graduated from MIT in 1996, and joined the faculty of art at Carnegie Mellon University. Today, he still performs in the medium of technology to audiences worldwide.

I like the question, "In your mind, is the computer just a tool?", because my answer is embedded in the question; I believe that mind and computer are coextensive. Of course, it is difficult to propose something like this without seeming addled by the trendy Gnostic philosophy of *The Matrix*, or caught in a swirly miasma of McLuhanisms about the "extensions of Man." But there is no doubt that software is more than an externalized record of thought (for which we already have writing). It seems to me that software is a living record of a thought one has had, or is having, about how the world ought to be. A brittle but determined little piece of mind that not only contains a model of one's point of view, but actively works to impose that view on the surrounding environment. If writing is a medium of thought, then software is an agent of will. When it executes my will, software and I form a single, coextensive unit of thought and purpose. The computer, accordingly, is merely the software's mortal coil.

Our intellects grow with our tools, eventually becoming inseparable. Although it may be hard to see how this could happen with a clunky item like the desktop PC, consider a much older tool: language. After a quarter of a million years of using language, our brains have actually evolved to accommodate it, and now have several substantial regions that are solely dedicated to processing it. Radical augmentations of human intellect like writing and computation, though much newer than spoken language, stand no less chance of becoming integrated into who we are, if our race survives long enough.

I believe computers represent a hybrid form of tool in that they combine the abilities of conventional tools to act on the world with the special attribute of tools like language and writing to enable substrata for thought. This combination makes the computer well suited for an integration with both our minds and bodies, to the point that it may someday sound as odd to ask the question, "Is the computer a tool?" as it is today to ask whether language is a tool.

With this in mind, the audience for my work varies considerably depending on the different contexts in which I present my projects. Like many people who create things, I enjoy publishing what I do on the web; my hope is that each of my Internet projects is somehow seen as a small gift to whomever might happen to stumble across it. I have only a faint idea of who my surfers might be; their traces through my sites tell me very little about them except, perhaps, statistically. For the most part, I would guess that many of the people who find my work on the web are students or practitioners of new-media art, which is to say, people like myself. But, judging from the quantity of bizarre emails in my inbox, I would also hesitate to generalize.

What is clear is that a visual culture has arisen, let us say since 1995 or so, in which artists and designers offer interactive abstractions in the online realm, and— perhaps for the same core reason that anybody looks to art at all—people really do consume them. The artists' justifications for these offerings are as varied as the projects themselves: Some are presented as modest formal experiments, others as technical demonstrations, and yet others as finished artworks or even calling-cards for their makers' design businesses. Whatever the reason, there seems to be a widespread interest in such abstract work, and a

number of splendid designers and artists have been able to find food for thought as a consequence of sharing their experiments in this peculiar economy of bartered abstract visual forms. I am thinking of artists like Lia, Danny Brown, James Tindall, Marius Watz, Manny Tan, and, of course, Martin Wattenberg, Yugo Nakamura and Joshua Davis. Whether by email or word of mouth, these artists, and many others like them, are engaged in a discourse with each other, sharing what they do in the hope that others find it interesting. They make new works as critical responses to previous ones. So, it is usually one of these colleagues whom I imagine experiencing my work, and whose critique I attempt to anticipate. These artists are exceptionally educated and sensitive observers, and also merciless critics. They are the audience I would like to have.

I do not present my work exclusively on the web because I enjoy sharing my work in person with other people. It was John Maeda who first pointed this out to me explicitly, when, sometime in 1999, he suggested that I ought to consider performance as a vehicle for my ideas about audiovisual abstraction. I am not certain that I would have realized my interest in new-media performance had he not prompted me. My first performance came at the invitation of Gerfried Stocker for the 2000 Ars Electronica festival, shortly after I graduated from the ACG, and I was immediately hooked by the intensity of communication I had with live observers. Since then, I have performed interactive projects at dozens of venues and festivals. It is an irregular living, but it has become my chief artistic outlet and my main way of getting by.

Joshua Davis

www.praystation.com

DYNAMIC ABSTRACTION MACHINE

Joshua Davis is an artist and technologist who lives in New York. Since the emergence of the web as an expressive medium, Davis has continued to define the "cutting edge" of digital youth culture.

Among modern artists, I conceptually identify with Jackson Pollock, not because I am a particular fan of his visual style, but because he always called himself a painter, even though a lot of the time his brush never hit the canvas. There is something in this disconnection—not using a brush or tool in traditional methods—that says a lot about the concept of dynamic abstraction; in that loss of control there can be a beauty in randomness.

Pollock might have argued that it is the process of abstraction that is dynamic, not the end result, which in his case was a static painting. In my own work, the end result is never static; by making room for as many anomalies as possible, I write programs that create unique compositions. I program the "brushes," the "paints," the "strokes," the rules, and the boundaries. However, it is the machine that generates the compositions: The programs draw themselves. I am in a constant state of surprise and discovery, because the program often compiles something I would never think of executing, or which would take me hours to create manually.

The program (or "machine," as I like to call it) is triggered simply by pressing the space bar on my keyboard. The random composition generators can populate a few hundred objects in the layout—imagine how long it would take if you had to do it by hand. Or, what if I kept asking you to give me a new composition, randomizing the assets, until you came up with a few hundred possible layouts?

Macromedia Flash is my primary piece of software. I know its limitations, but I very much like hacking it; it is just like finding new and different ways to use paint.

Basically, I am still the same artist I was as a painter, only my tools have changed. Fundamentally, art and design have been taught as very static processes: executing style and method to arrive at an end result. I am rewriting the rules, redefining the process.

I create for an audience of one—myself. No-one else has to understand, like or "get" my work. This might seem odd considering I have chosen a medium that is open to a global audience and through which I share my work with others. If other people do not like what I produce, that is OK; if they do like it, it is an added bonus. I know I am creating work for the love of making it, rather than because I think people will like it.

My work is malleable: I can write programs for the Net, I can capture movements for use in video or DVD broadcast, and I can run programs through a PostScript Driver to capture the composition the program generated for use in print. One process, multiple media.

For me, the artform is not the few days it takes me to write the program; it is the few weeks I will spend living with the work, waiting for the work to evolve. Pressing the space bar, pressing the space bar, always waiting to capture that moment in time: the beautiful accident.

From: "John Maeda"
Hi Joshua,

Thanks.
Can you answer the question is the computer a tool and, if so, how is it a tool?

From: "Joshua Davis"

yeah I know,

I wasn't really interested in answering that question—I feel the answer is simple and there is nothing really to elaborate on. It is a tool, and I treat it just like I would a paintbrush or pencil.

6. Physical

When I lived in Japan, I had the fortune of taking a break from computers. I was attending an art school where there were few computing resources, an intentional move on my part. The period was pre-web and, therefore, pre-Google. Desiring to find something new to me that quite often turned out to be about something old, I found myself regularly in the library. It contained an unusually strong collection of books on kinetic art, which I attributed to a prominent contemporary sculptor who taught at the school, Morio Shinoda, a pioneer of avant-garde kinetic sculpture.

I took Shinoda's class on plastic form and held in great admiration his dry approach to interpersonal communication. Always puffing on a cigarette that appeared glued to his mouth, Shinoda often seemed more interested in the wispy patterns of smoke than in the conversation around him. Something of a Japanese Clint Eastwood, he was someone you felt naturally afraid to approach, but one day I found the courage to ask the master about his mysterious departure from the kinetic art scene decades earlier. Why did he choose to pursue more conventional sculpture in his later years? Was it because he felt the world was in flux after the advent of the rocket age and/or advances in video as a new artistic medium? What epic movement or moment forced his interests away from kinetic art? Trembling with excitement, I hoped at long last to solve a mystery not explained on the library's shelves.

Shinoda took a deep hit of his cigarette and looked to the sky, paused, then in a surprisingly colorful, un-Japanese manner said, "Because it was a bitch." My raised eyebrows belied my sincere surprise. He continued, "The shit broke down too often. I'd sell it, and then immediately would have to travel to some place to repair it. So I got out of that business fast." Expecting an eloquent pearl of ancient artistic wisdom, I got a coarse reply from a mouth that needed to be washed out with soap and water. But, as the years passed and I made my own brand of kinetic art on the computer, every so often I would recall that moment and reflect on how right the master really was – foul language and all.

Technology eventually breaks down, and the more technology you use, the sooner it fails to work. So, Shinoda's later sculptures were made with thick aluminum sheets, aircraft cable, and solid brass pigs that never "crashed," creating a purity of timelessness mediated by a selection of proper materials. Shinoda's good business sense should not be underestimated either as he was no longer required to run a twenty-four-hour technical support line.

Is any art truly timeless? Does any art deserve to last forever? Consider recent well-intentioned efforts to archive and preserve digital media art. Computer codes are designed to run on specific computers; therefore, with new computers released and made obsolete within the same month, maintaining all computer artworks would require keeping every model of computer ever developed. There have been attempts to do this, but they are probably futile. What determines that a computer artwork should live forever when there are mountains and streams that are routinely destroyed by humanity? Why should digital art be any more powerful and important than nature?

Due to modern information technology, we are at a moment in time when the very meaning of "now" implies a global instance. In my mind, the challenge today is to seek to extend the "now" to better savor the moment inside ourselves – the world will be affected soon enough. Technological events are set in motion that will affect our virtual future, but I treasure my physical present.

Interactions between the virtual and the physical worlds are popular today in so-called ubiquitous computing scenarios. My students' initial take on this area may at first appear frivolous; but, really, what is more important than eating?

EDIBLE VIRTUAL REALITY
Elise Co, 1998

A prerequisite for physical life, besides having a physical form, is nourishment. Often, eating is more than a means of survival, becoming a passion in its own right. Co's favorite breakfast—cranberry pancakes and sourdough toast washed down with an orange drink—is immortalized as an interactive visual experience. Each click represents a bite, and each virtual bite results in a gastronomic reaction that is visualized with simple 2-D graphics.

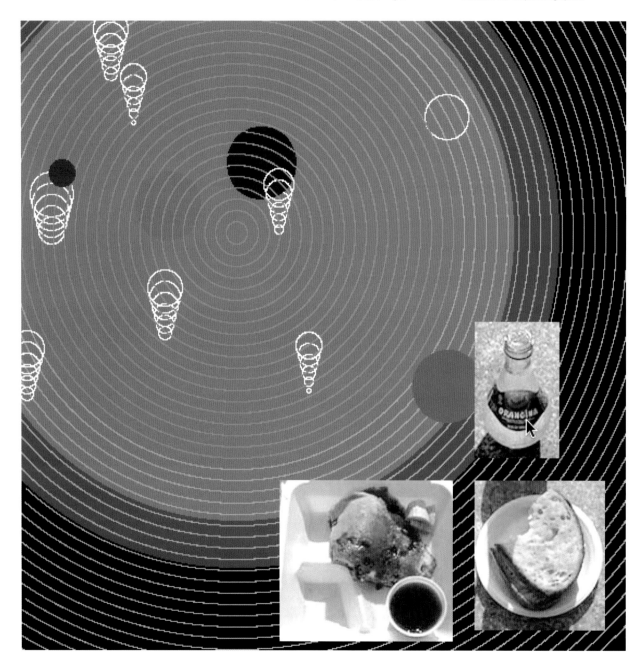

The computer-controlled laser cutter will most certainly be the laser printer of the twenty-first century. Laser-engraving such information as stock details, poetry, and family photos onto fruit and vegetables demonstrates the lighter side of laser light.

Photograph by Webb Chappell

DISSOLVE THEM CLUMPS
Tom White, 1998

I have never sampled a Malt-o-Meal breakfast, but I am told by Tom White that this piece is just as good as the real thing. Removing the clumps of powder appears to be the goal in this appetite-whetting interaction.

IF I HAD A HUNDRED-DOLLAR BILL
Tom White, 1998

A fantasy piece by White realizes every late-night, hard-working student's (and professor's) dream of getting anything you want from the local vending machine. Placing a hundred-dollar bill in the slot releases a thrilling junk-food heaven without any of the calories.

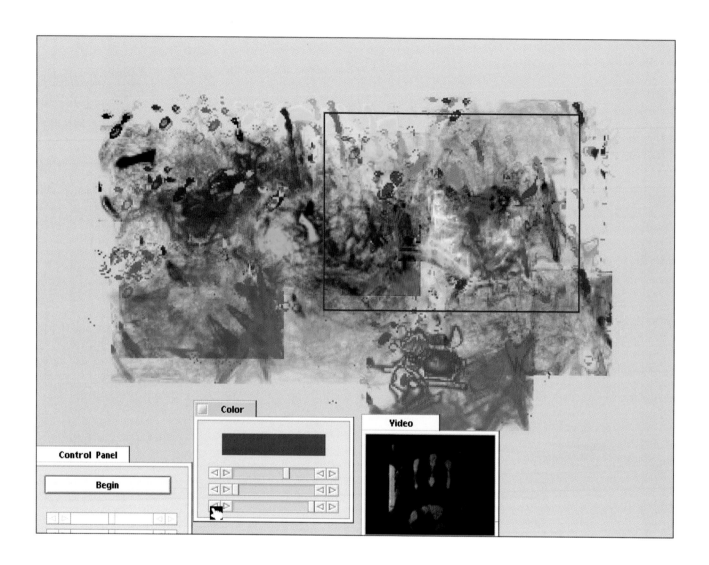

DIGITAL FINGER PAINTING
Tom White, 1997

To achieve the squishy sensation of finger painting, White rigs up a simple interface comprising a medical bladder and some soy sauce. He delivers a close approximation to fiddling with wet paint whilst on a dry computer.

POETIC TYPE FLOW PROJECTED ON POOL OF WATER
David Small and Tom White, 1997

Small and White collaborated to produce
this runaway interactive hit, which combines
White's squishy pad with Small's elegant
dynamic typography. A projection of flowing
text on water is disrupted by pressure input
from the surface of the hand. The calming effect
of this piece has proven to be an elusive quality
to emulate in any such interactive installation in
the world to date.

Photograph by Webb Chappell

153

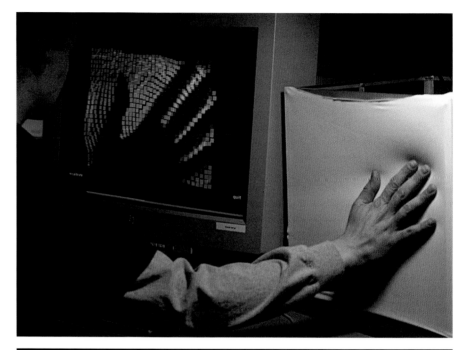

FABRIC INTERFACE
Bill Keays, 1997

Keays uses a soft canvas interface as the input device in this project. This simple technique seems to resurface every few years, but the moment when video sensing will literally be in real time is always a few years away.

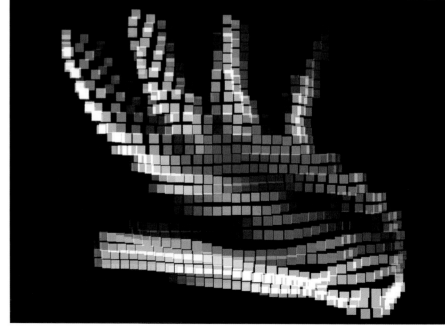

SEE-THROUGH PERSON
Elise Co, 1999

Hand-threading over six hundred individual
fiber-optic strands into arrays attached to the
front and back of her body, Co attained a small
area of transparency through her body. Here,
she is waving her hand behind her back, which,
incredibly, is visible from the front.

VIRTUAL BACK ON BACKPACK
Elise Co, 1999

A portable LCD backpack enabled Co to input arm movement and breath to trigger flowing, visual reactions in the phantasmagorical computer-graphic analog to her physical back.

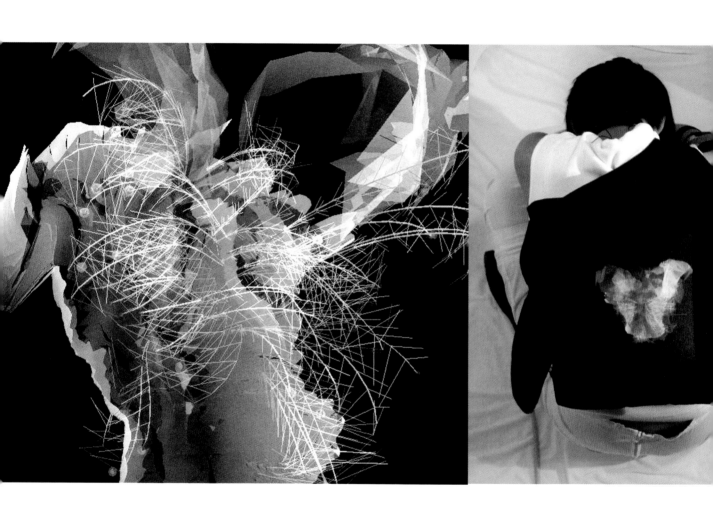

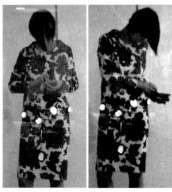

SYSTEM OF COMMUNICATING LIGHTS
Elise Co, 1999

A system of lit elements intercommunicate and form pulsating rhythms of light that are mediated by wireless interventions using a Palm hand-held computing device.

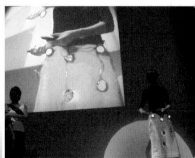

REACTIVE BOXES
Casey Reas, 2000

Metal protrusions move according to the
input received from a remote computer. This
prickliness on the otherwise sleek box suggests
an insectlike characteristic that at first produces
a sense of discomfort, but is followed by a
comfortable feeling of fascination.

A delayed reaction to a strong stimulus is often the best approach to adopt in life, unless of course you are in danger. These twin boxes are slow to respond, one to sound, the other to light. The latter sits on my desk at work and at an indeterminate moment spins its arms for a brief while to discharge the energy it has stored. I am thus constantly reminded of Casey Reas.

Casey Reas

MOBILE ROBOT A LA MODULATOR
Casey Reas, 2000

For his graduating work, Reas crafted an
ambitious human-sized robotic piece as an
exercise in light, mass, motion, and sensing.
A cross between a lantern and a manatee,
Trundle is evidence that all handcrafted
constructions not only indelibly bear the
mark of their creator's hands but his or her
personality as well.

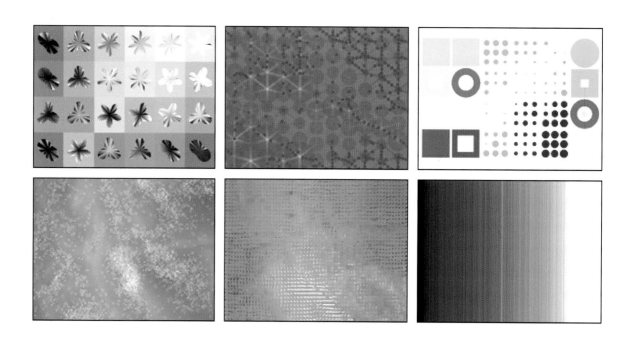

VIDEO INPUT BEGETS VIDEO OUTPUT FOREVER
Aesthetics and Computation Group, 2000

The Introspection Machine was a group project that combined all the members' talents into an ecosystem of visual input and output. A system of video cameras and CRTs became the primary subject of an abstract computational process with no meaning beyond the system itself.

Pictured on the right is the hurried process of assembling the piece for display, which, I believe, often reveals the real reason for anyone to make art: self discovery.

Combining a tea strainer and discarded
desk lamp, Pashenkov creates a hemispheric
information display from many manually
soldered LED elements. This primitive display
marked the beginning of various avenues of
research into simply configured light devices.

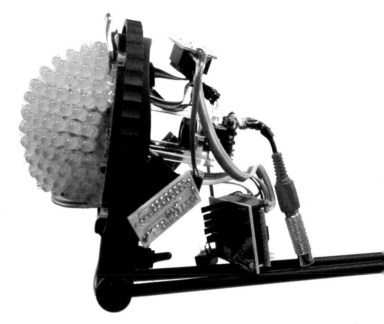

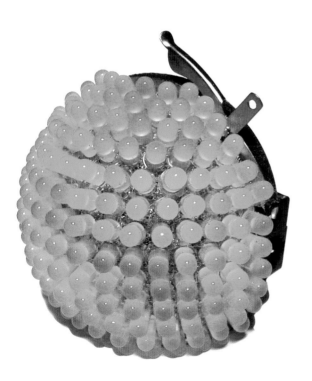

BATTERY-SIZED TEXT LANTERN
Nikita Pashenkov, 2001

Reducing his light experiments into a palm-
sized form, Pashenkov creates a message
flashlight that is a powerful expression of the
shifting balance between electrical power and
physical form. The form is expressed by the
dominant element of the battery.

POCKETABLE LOW-RESOLUTION VIDEO DISPLAY
Megan Galbraith, Simon Greenwold, Justin Manor, 2001

A collaboration between students resulted in a reduced-resolution hand-held appliance for carrying short video clips anywhere.

POINT-TO-POINT VISIBLE COMMUNICATION
Simon Greenwold, 2002

Adapting the theme of laser tag, Greenwold's
handy units transmit words instead of death.
Pulses of laser light send a kind of Morse code
between the units, resulting in your favorite
word being displayed on the screen on the top
of the devices.

COMPUTATIONAL FASHION DESIGN ELEMENT
Megan Galbraith, 2002

The question of how to rapidly prototype physical systems was addressed by Galbraith in her creation of a simple computing platform on which to "program" fashion items. Galbraith has produced a dynamic handbag, a reactive top, and interactive pants.

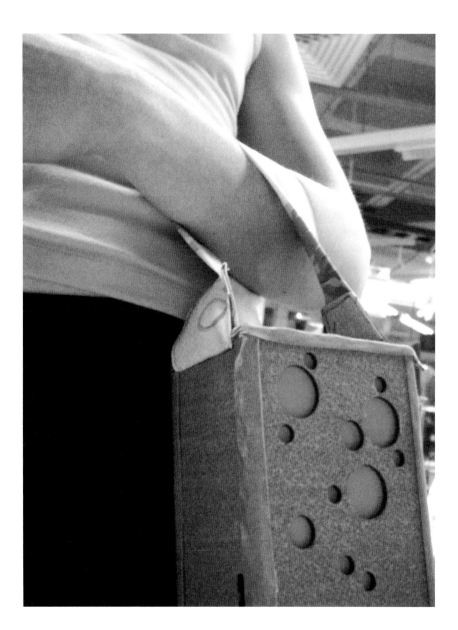

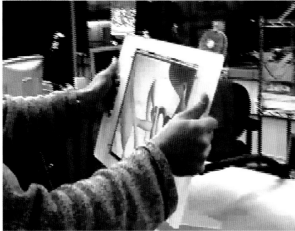

WINDOW INTO A QUASI-VIRTUAL QUASI-PHYSICAL SPACE
Simon Greenwold, 2001

Within a month of his arrival, Greenwold had conceived a prototype of a system for constructing augmented realities. Objects are built using a 3-D sensor and are then viewed within the actual physical space by grasping the window and moving it around.

LOW-COST THREE-DIMENSIONAL SCANNING SYSTEM
Simon Greenwold, 2001

The closing door to the ACG was the door of a refrigerator; to be more specific, a mini fridge with an over-sized LCD for the door and a low-cost 3-D scanning technology invented by Greenwold. Objects are placed in the fridge, which scans their physical form and creates a digital model. The bridge between physical and virtual reality was finally met in the unexpected form of this household appliance. Had we known this at the beginning of the ACG, we may have been better off naming the group the Aesthetics and Refrigeration Group.

Elise Co

www.mintymonkey.com
BEYOND PIXELS

Elise Co graduated from MIT in 2000, and moved to Switzerland to join the University of Art and Design Basel. Co is now a freelance designer based in the Los Angeles area.

When I imagine what a computer will be like in the future, I find it hard to predict specific components or sets of capabilities because I believe that its input, output and processing possibilities are boundless. I do not wonder whether computers will be able to do X or Y, because I am sure they will be able to. Instead, I consider their position in the world, especially how they might be situated in relation to humans. What kinds of stimuli will they use to affect us? What will be the means by which we affect them through control, programming or interaction?

Recently, I found myself in pursuit of a glowing sky and a lit-up sea. Not man-made creations, the northern lights and bioluminescent plankton are natural phenomena based on electrical and chemical properties that have already been reproduced in current technology. In the first, charged particles from solar wind enter the earth's magnetosphere, are guided by the magnetic field towards the polar atmosphere, and strike atoms of gas. These excited atoms emit excess energy as photons, producing visible light that can be seen as a shifting glow in the night-time sky. The second example involves a similar emission of excess energy as photons; in this case, a chemical reaction within an organism creates the highly charged compound luciferin (the basic substrate of any bioluminescent reaction). Planktonic dinoflagellates (unicellular protists that exhibit a great diversity of form) and bacteria naturally luminesce in this fashion, emitting stronger light when disturbed. So, when present in large enough numbers in the sea, they turn the water into a reactive volume that illuminates breaking waves, surf, wakes, and other turbulences.

Man-made light-emitting devices, including CRTs, LCD backlights, and electroluminescent (EL) panels, follow the same general rule of charging a compound (a phosphor) to an excited state to produce visible light. Every display pixel we see is based on this principle. Yet, the way we experience this unexpected luminescence in nature (as a natural phenomena) is totally different from how we experience it via computers in our daily lives (on a synthetic level). We receive the same basic stimulus—dynamic, interactive light—but the quality of the effect it has on us is vastly different. This is not news to anyone, but I think it is interesting to look at the overlaps and interplays of a natural versus a synthetic experience.

Computers are not necessarily monolithic boxes anymore. They are devices: cell phones, pagers, PDAs, laptops and PCs. They are things we carry or put on tables, and every device has its accompanying cable, stylus, power supply, and so on. Everything is self-contained; computers are entities. Interacting with so many devices inevitably involves focusing and staring at an object instead of just looking into space or feeling things in the environment. When we encounter the northern lights or glowing plankton, we appreciate them as specific phenomena, but we also understand that they exist as manifestations within larger complex systems: weather patterns, migration, tides, space. Computers are not there to create ambience; we want them to perform tasks and relay data, and so they (usually) cannot be formless blobs with indecipherable pulsations. Much of what is so enticing about natural phenomena—the mystery, the unpredictability—is contrary to what we want from machines. However, I think we should start to think of machines less as boxes of practicality and more as generic control mechanisms for mediating all kinds of interactions and stimuli. It is also exciting to imagine computers taking on some of the qualities of natural systems by diversifying and, through autonomy and interconnectivity, forming larger dynamic systems.

Sensorially, the things we encounter in nature are much more complex than the things people tend to generate on the computer. Often it is a mark of programming prowess to make something that seems organic; simulations of the natural world (whether lighting, form or motion) are benchmarks of how sophisticated technology has become. Synthetic things certainly have their own appeal, and I do not think the point is to mimic nature, but we are drawn to complexity and texture in the natural world. Maybe it is this ambiguity and texture that we miss in the computational world. The way we use computers now—to transmit and process particular data—requires precise and high-content inputs and outputs. But, as machines become more ubiquitous and appropriate for less task-oriented situations, there will be a lot of room for inputs or outputs that are not as exact or as efficient but that appeal to a much broader sensory range or provide a more evocative experience. I like the idea of explicit encounters giving way to reconfigurable form, shifting texture, irregular surface, vapors and gases.

Technology in the future is a wide-open space, and it is easy to extrapolate from a single pixel a whole ecosystem of electronic devices. The pace of technology makes it easy to imagine almost anything. I do not doubt that computers will have wheels or wings or tastes or smells, but the real question is not so much how we will interact with individual devices, but how they fit into our world and our own personal ecologies of life.

172 Physical

Daniel Rozin

fargo.itp.tsoa.nyu.edu/~danny
PHYSICAL COMPUTING

Daniel Rozin is an interactive artist and developer living in New York. He is also one of the key faculty members of the New York University Interactive Telecommunications Program. Using his rare mixture of skills, Rozin creates digital mirrors and windows in endless varieties.

It is quite obvious that in the future the act of computation will not be confined to computers but will occur in many physical objects. This idea of combining digital computation and physical objects is often referred to as "physical computing."

By definition, this new field comprises two very different disciplines. Computation, with its origins in mathematics, is a very pure, theoretical and liberated form, without many constraints and limitations. Creators of computational media are restricted mainly by their imagination and skill, and can expect their creations to work forever. The physical part of physical computing, on the other hand, is an area governed by limitation, the laws of physics, cost, wear and tear, and the unpredictability of the real world.

The people working in physical computing also come from these two disciplines. They either started off creating software but saw the advantage of adding physicality to their work to achieve a more intuitive and easy way for people to interact with it; or they began by creating objects but recognized the benefits of adding a level of logic and computation to their creations. In general, the latter group of people are happier about this combination as it elevates their creations to new heights, while the former are usually unhappy about the limitations, difficulty and simplicity of physical objects.

Software design and the design of physical objects are generally very different. Software projects tend to end up being very complex and multi-layered. The process of developing them is typically one of addition. A kernel of functional ability is defined and then built upon with the addition of features and interfaces. When designing a functional physical object, the main process is one of subtraction. Beginning with a wide and ambitious brief for what an object should do, designers often produce a much simpler design that can actually be built and prove reliable. As a result, physical objects are generally simple and more intuitive to operate.

The field of physical object design has a rich and proud heritage: generations of thinkers and designers, and centuries of trial and error. Software design, conversely, has a poor tradition that is best ignored (no-one is very proud of MS DOS or the command line as a design achievement).

Clearly, combining two such different disciplines into one form is not going to be a seamless effort; indeed, early attempts were usually biased toward one or the other approach. What I am awaiting for is the emergence of a new type of designer, one who is comfortable enough in both components of physical computing to develop an intuition that is unique to this form, and who is skillful enough to take advantage of both its aspects.

We know the future holds the integration of computation into everyday objects. We already have the technology to achieve such ubiquity. What we still lack is a new discipline of design that, rather than repackage designs from the fields of software or physical design, takes advantage of the possibilities and creates new experiences in a unique form.

☺ Avert misunderstanding by calm,
poise and balance. ☺

7. Education

The first class I taught at MIT was probably the best I have ever administered. You might think that as you become more experienced you become a better teacher. I may possibly have improved with age, but there is something special about the first time you teach in a new environment. The rules of engagement are completely undefined between teacher and student, both sides are allowed to demand more than expected. There is no precedent to limit the kind and extent of learning that can occur. I see this whenever I visit a new school.

Teaching can also be very tedious. To regurgitate the same ideas at the same hour on the same day of the week during the same period of the year for the rest of your life is a form of intellectual torture. Worse, your waning interest in the learning material can never be concealed from students. To be a boring teacher who is bored with teaching is to be scorned by the students whose enlightenment you are charged with providing. I wish it were the case that if this befell you, you would lose your job, but the reality is that you can continue in perpetuity because of the educational system's imperfect structures. Yet, were it not for this flaw in the system, I certainly should have been fired in the past.

Over the years, my own teachers have criticized me for jumping between fields and interests. Having grown up at MIT, turning from a machine-vision understudy to a parallel-computer programmer to a semiconductor device simulation person, only to end up years later with a career in the arts and design, is testament to my lifelong problem. I have managed to stay on course (or, more accurately, "off" course) because of a piece of wisdom relayed to me by the legendary designer and artist Takenobu Igarashi, who explained that life could be lived broadly as an Eastern or Western quest for knowledge.

The Eastern approach advocates breadth of knowledge; the Western position concentrates on a single axis of knowledge. Igarashi describes the process of aging as building a mountain of knowledge: In the Eastern way, the mountain becomes broad and slowly rises from the earth; the Western path piles knowledge upon knowledge, rising quickly, like a pyre into the sky. His point is that the older you grow in the Eastern approach, the broader and more stable your mountain becomes, like the famously symmetrical Mount Fuji. By reaching for the sky without enough breadth of exploration, Igarashi argued, the thin but steep mountain can easily fall to the ground if just one piece of knowledge fails you in the precipitously stacked Western way. Recently, a professor at Rensallear University commented: "But, when the thin mountain falls over, often the mistake is understood and new shoots of knowledge grow out of the fallen pile's remains." I realized then that either way is fine, breadth or focus, as long as you learn from your mistakes.

My period of uncertainty about my reason for teaching, instead of solely concentrating on making new work, came to an end one summer. I had gone, for the third year running, to Maine College of Art as a guest lecturer on designer and typographer Wolfgang Weingart's summer course. I watched him give his introductory lecture, the same one he had given there the previous two years, and I wondered how bored Weingart must be to recite the same lecture for decades. Suddenly, a switch turned on in my head; I noticed something slightly different about this third lecture, and then I understood the pattern: Each time Weingart gave the lecture, it was infinitesimally simpler than the last, the concepts were delivered in an incrementally purer form. Thus, I saw that over many years Weingart had continually flattened his mountain of knowledge into such a perfectly broad structure that it appeared level and unnoticeable. This guise of "nothingness" hid the fact that Weingart's mountain was so completely merged with the general plane of knowledge that the mountain did not matter. What mattered was his existence on a plane that reached outwards in all directions to infinity.

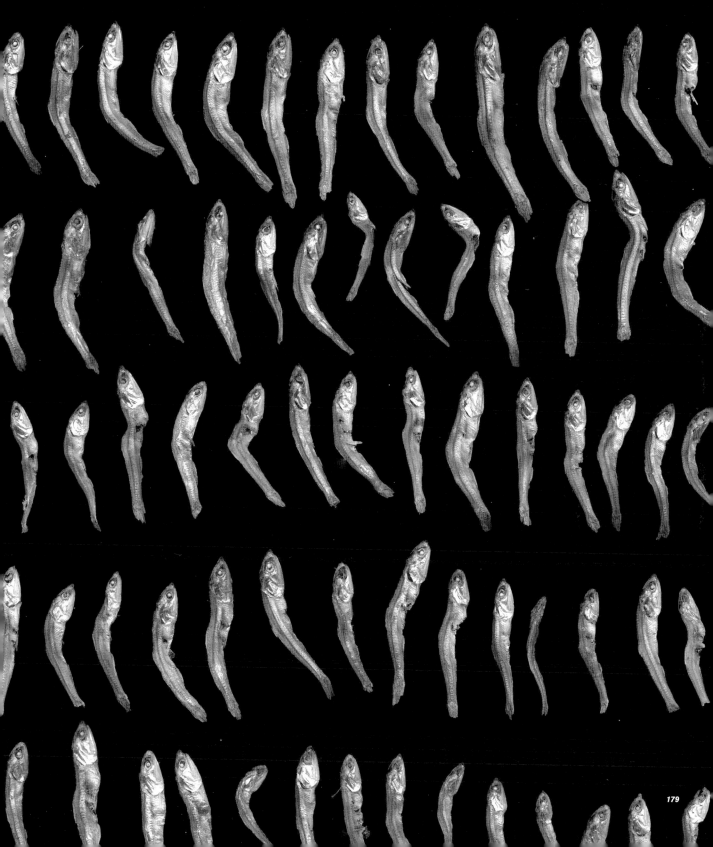

In this chapter, I present my fondest recollections of rediscovering the computer with students shortly after my arrival at MIT.

VARIATION IN CIRCLES DERIVED FROM A SINGLE CLICK
Peter Cho, 1996

This exercise explores the variation available when limited to working with circles and monochrome graphics. Depending on where you click on the screen, different but similar patterns emerge. The bold use of space and oddly shaped striped bands of black and white evoke a literal but abstract experience.

Tiongson produced an interactive composition using circles. Each click tunnels the user deeper into the corresponding circle. The circle within a circle motif reveals a classic computer-science theme, recursion, which hints at the infinite conceptual space of the computer.

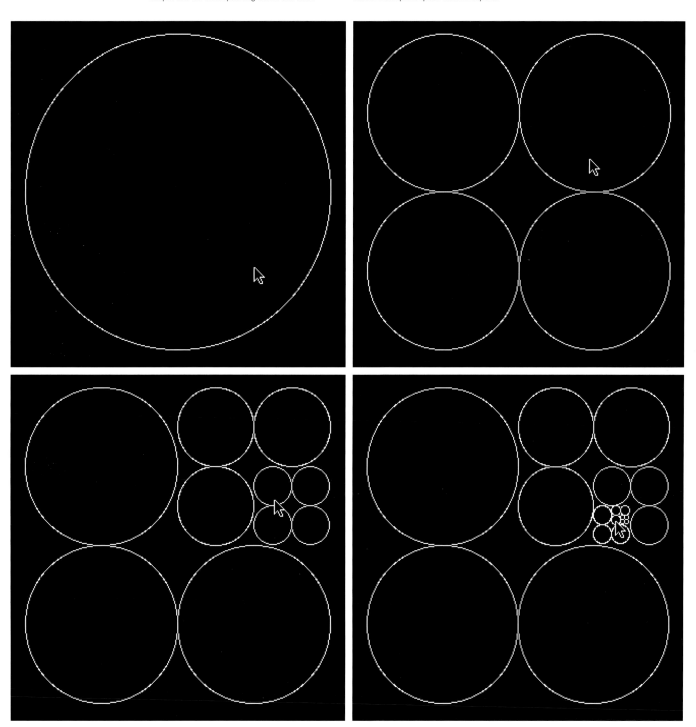

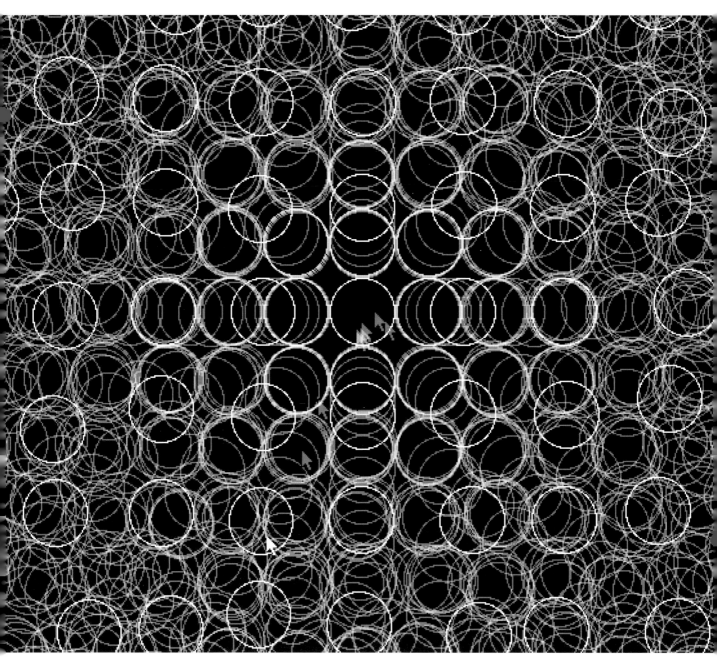

CHAOS TO ORDER
Robert Poor, 1996

Poor's composition of circles is positioned erratically if clicked at the edge of the display, and in a more orderly manner if clicked nearer to the center. Initial work by students relied too much on random noise, so afterward such techniques were forbidden in all classwork.

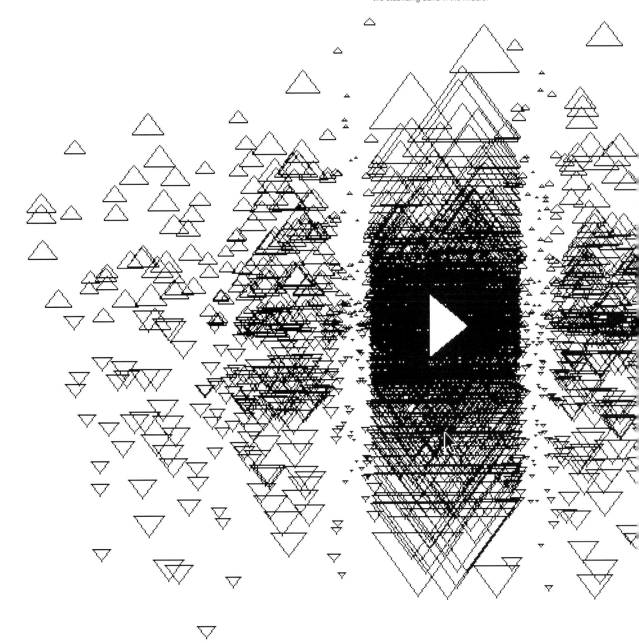

ORDERED CHAOS
Reed Kram, 1996

This rhythmic pattern using triangles in an overtly random manner was completed before I outlawed randomness. The exaggerated variety of triangle size, from pixel-scale to prominent visibility, is nonetheless successful because of the stabilizing band in the middle.

With the aim of expressing balance using a
single shape, three triangles are repeatedly
interrelated based on the position of the
cursor. A balance is achieved in the imbalance
of the triangles' sizes, perhaps due in part to
the triangles formed in the negative space.

DYNAMIC BALANCE AS THREE TRIANGLES
Peter Cho, 1996

CODEPENDENT INTERACTION OF CIRCLES
Tom White, 1996

Attentive circles track the position of the cursor
in anti-symmetrical directions. A slight sense
of vertigo is achieved by the synchronous
movements of the circular elements.

Gorbet's assignment in balance revealed his interpretations of a state of equilibrium. In this piece, a dynamic mobile is awarded new weights each time the mouse is clicked. Each square's weight is proportional to its size, and produces a state of imbalance that is visualized dynamically. The system comes to rest when balance is achieved around the center element. I was pleased to have confirmed in this high-quality work my high expectations about Gorbet.

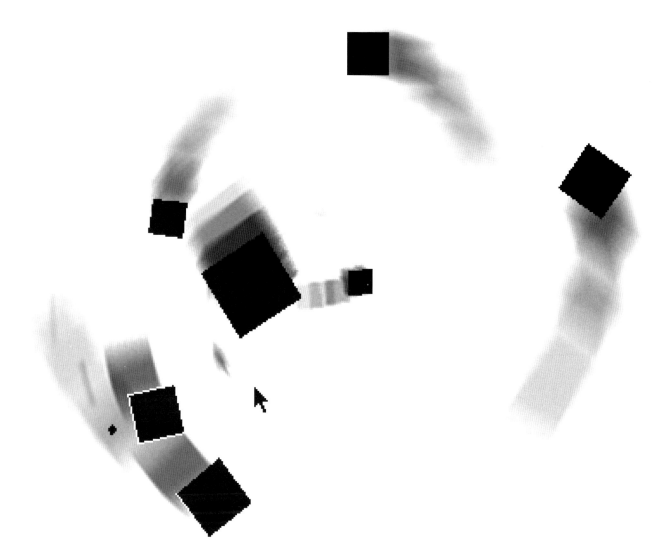

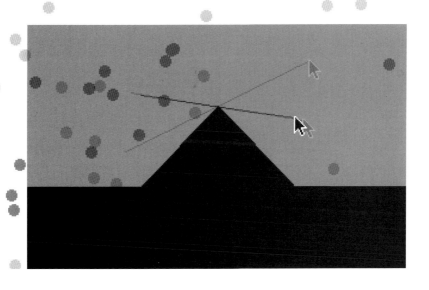

MANUAL BALANCE OF LOCAL AND GLOBAL SPACE
Tom White, 1996

Visualizing balance in a literal way, White places a line atop a primitive fulcrum. Moving the line up and down incurs an imbalance in the population of dots overlaid on the screen. The juxtaposition of these two unrelated elements is surprising but not discordant.

TWO SQUARES INTERRUPTING SPACE

Peter Cho, 1996

This deceptively simple interaction expresses the relationship between two plain squares that are continuously brought together through the mathematical operation of XOR. The shapes are quickly obscured in a kind of noise wrought purely from their own interactions.

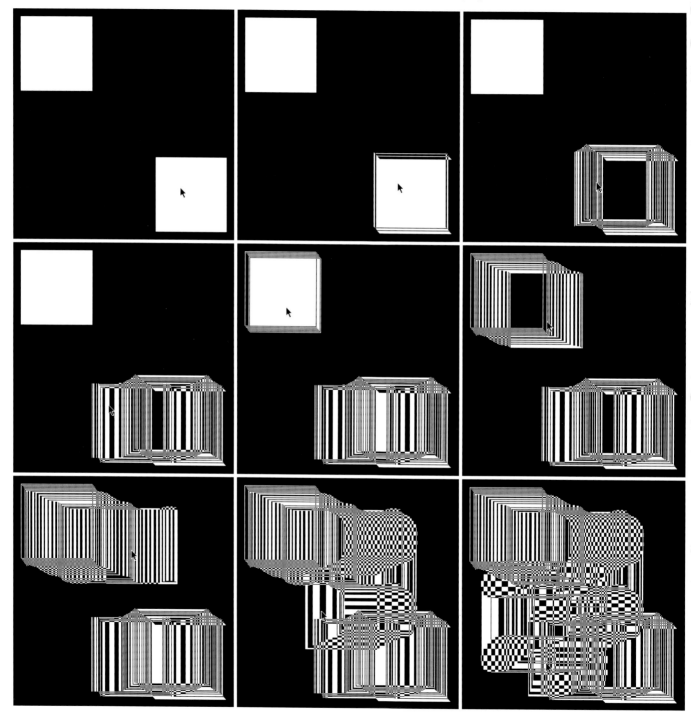

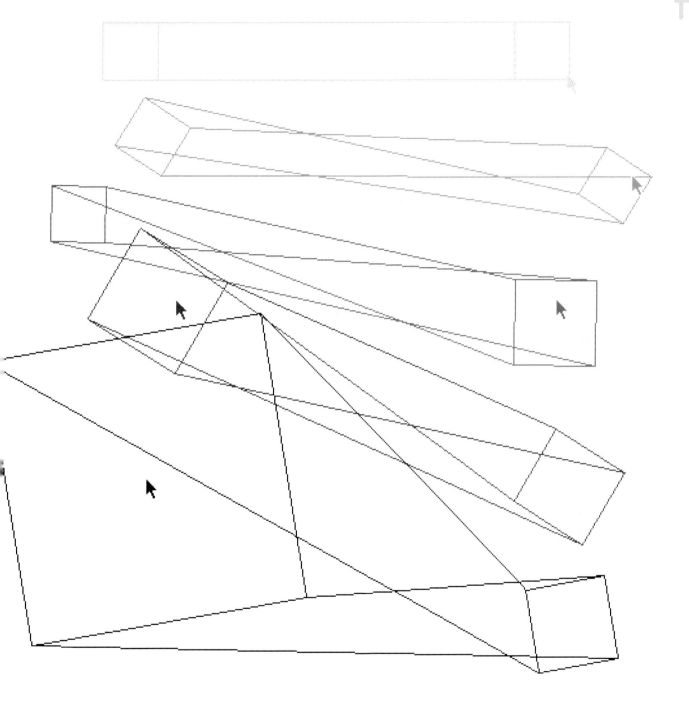

Kram produces an interactive anomaly in his piece. Two squares are interlinked in such a way that if one square is moved, the other also moves in a similar manner but with a delayed response. The smooth but subtle interplay between the squares served as a key reference for future work that focused on such physically inspired motions.

DYNAMIC INTERCONNECTEDNESS
Reed Kram, 1996

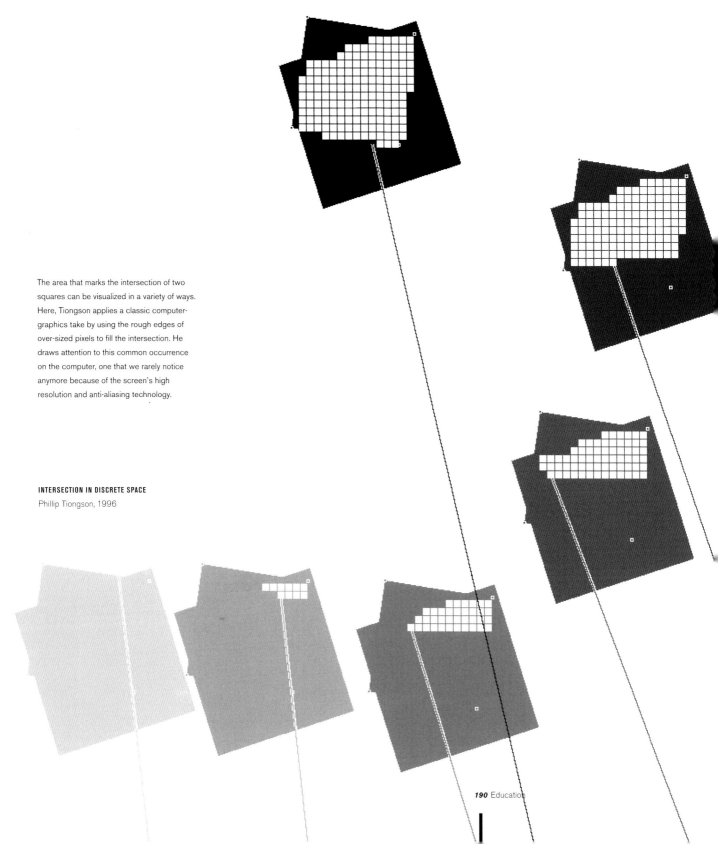

The area that marks the intersection of two squares can be visualized in a variety of ways. Here, Tiongson applies a classic computer-graphics take by using the rough edges of over-sized pixels to fill the intersection. He draws attention to this common occurrence on the computer, one that we rarely notice anymore because of the screen's high resolution and anti-aliasing technology.

INTERSECTION IN DISCRETE SPACE
Phillip Tiongson, 1996

The union of two squares is visualized in a straightforward manner: the casual yet sublime shadow. This simple mechanism immediately transports the unified area into the graphic domain, implementing a subjective response from an objective situation.

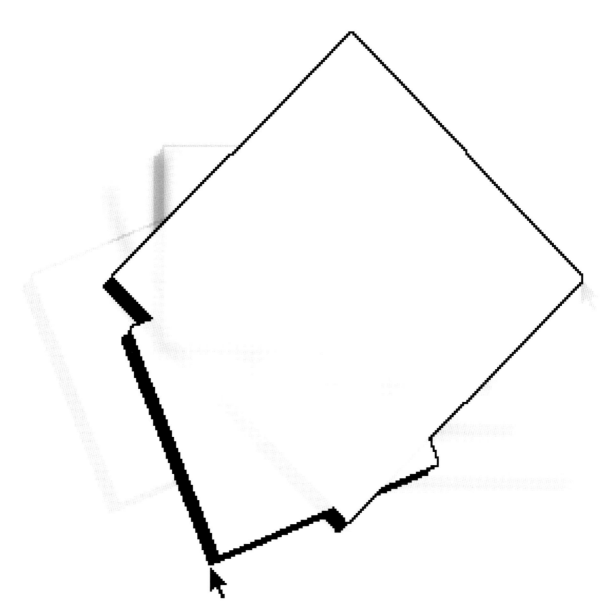

TWO POINTS LITERALLY CHAINED TOGETHER

Matthew Grenby, 1996

The most obvious way to connect two points
in space is a line. Grenby demonstrates strong
illustration skills with a ball-and-chain rendering
system that effectively uses a figurative
technique to concretize an abstract concept.

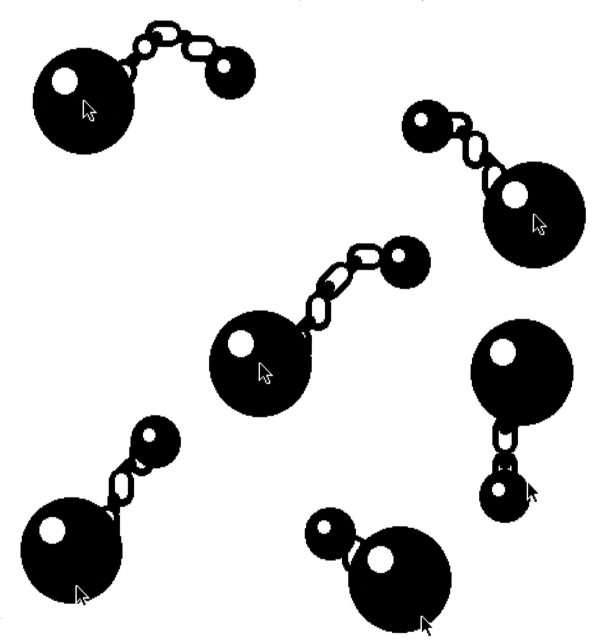

Phillip Tiongson, 1996

Tiongson affirms his warm-hearted personality
with a smiley generator that takes any two
points and creates a smile near the two "eyes"
formed by the points. Multiple clicks create an
unanticipated network of leftover smiles.

Aesthetics and Computation Group

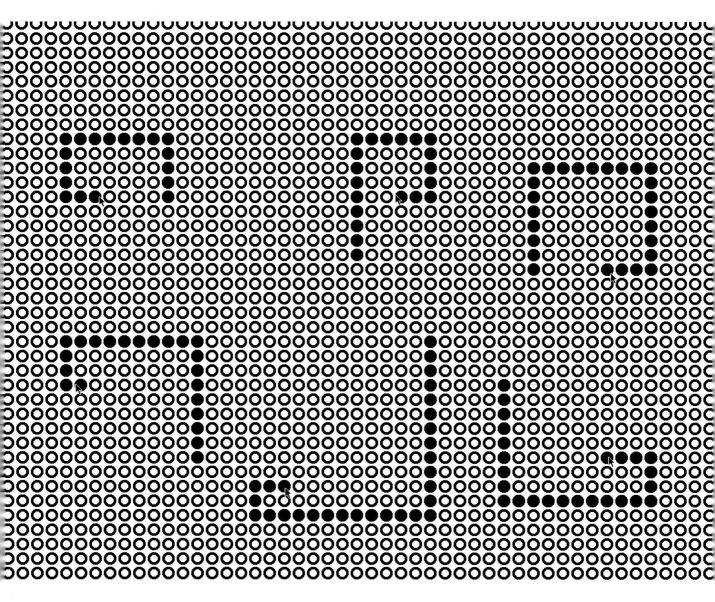

THE LONGER DISTANCE BETWEEN TWO POINTS

Nelson Minar, 1996

Although the shortest distance between two points is a line, Minar's program generates a more circuitous path between two points. Visual mischief of this caliber will always attract the right kind of attention.

SUCCESSIVE REFINEMENTS IN CONNECTEDNESS
Nelson Minar, 1996

When two points are clicked on Minar's canvas,
a connection is formed in the brief time span
of half a second. A coarse connection of large
pixels is immediately rendered between the
two points, which rapidly evolves into smaller
pixels placed at a finer pitch. This imagery
accurately depicts a slowed-down moment
of computer processing that can be better
appreciated by the human eye.

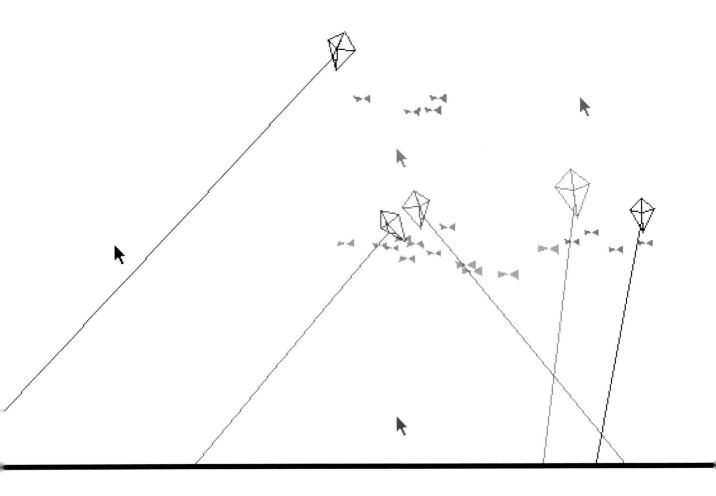

GO FLY A KITE
Robert Poor, 1996

As a quick exercise in interaction design, I asked
students to create kites. Kites are traditionally
operated by tugging on a string, a method
that I felt would translate well to mouse-driven
dynamic graphics. Poor created a kite, complete
with a stream of ribbons, that is brought closer
or let out further by moving the mouse to the
left and right.

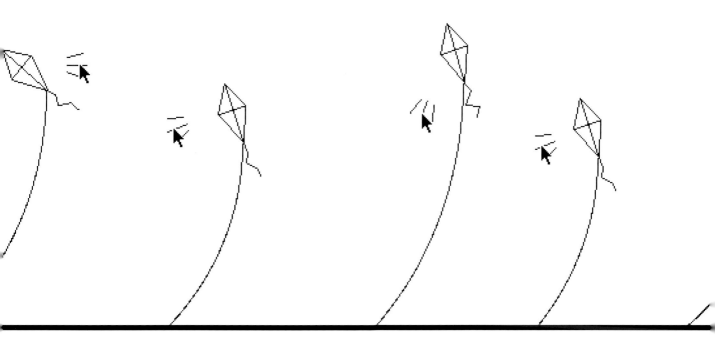

BLOW AWAY KITE
Peter Cho, 1996

The kite exercise as interpreted by Cho uses the mouse to summon the wind. Each click releases a small puff of wind that guides the kite's position on the screen.

BLAST-AWAY KITE
Reed Kram, 1996

A click of the mouse launches a shockwave that
disturbs the swaying kite. The instant when the
shockwave makes contact with the kite and the
moment after impact define a dramatic moment
of indirect manipulation.

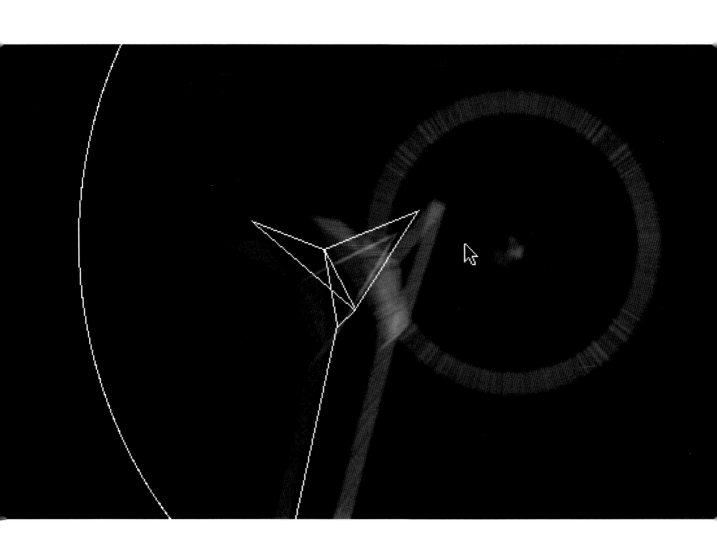

Tiongson turns the notion of flying a kite on its head by visualizing the flight from the kite's perspective. As you fly this kite, you especially notice the joy of the person toward whose hands you are guided.

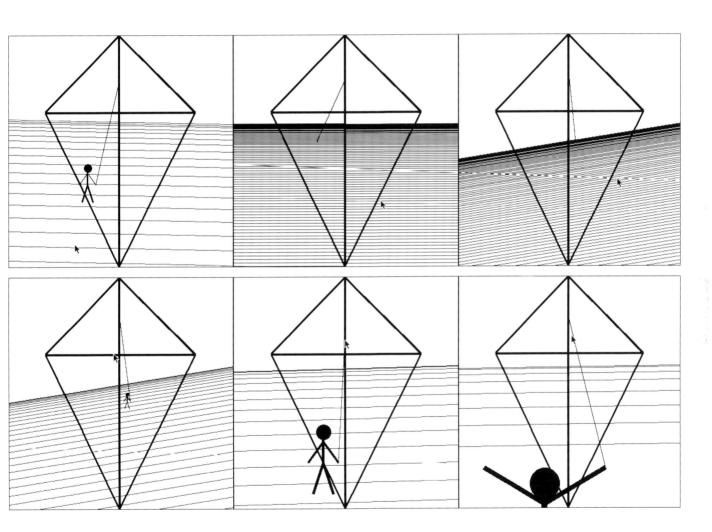

The network is a useful method for bringing everyone together, whether they like it or not. Here, mouse clicks are visualized in a variety of ways, ranging from the nonsensical to the beautiful, by a set of unique software clients.

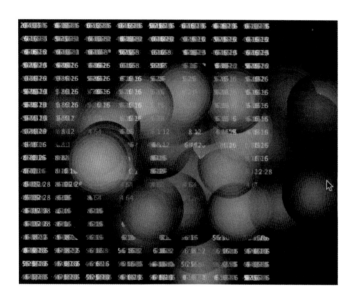

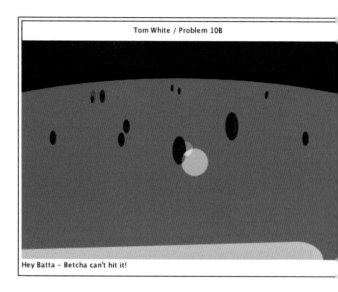

MANY NUMBERS
Joey Berzowska, 1996

BATTER UP
Tom White, 1996

Mouse clicks are converted into numerical pairs and an associated sphere-shaped graphic. As each click enters the space, the numbers continue to flow vertically à la *Matrix*, but this was conceived long before the movie entered popular consciousness.

White takes all the mouse clicks and dispatches them to a baseball video game of his own design. This whimsical interpretation of what are literally just a set of points in space shows the kind of devious imagination that lurks in all of us.

Ideally, a sense of community is encouraged in the classroom. In the most competitive of schools, however, there is little possibility for such feelings to emerge. I have a mini theory that since team sports are not usually the favorite of truly individual minds, team-building will be prevented in some of the best schools. Therefore, I have taken to watching football and basketball games to get a better sense of this environment and psyche. Go team!

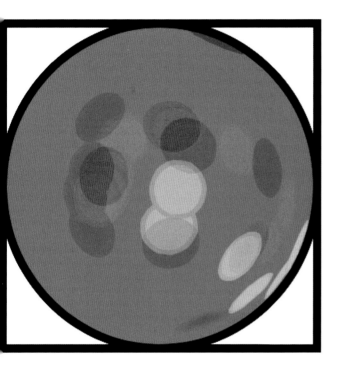

GENTLE IMPLICATION OF A LARGER SPACE
Reed Kram, 1996

GOD AS THE CLIENT
Nelson Minar, 1996

Each click is softly projected onto the surface of a sphere as a slowly fading and rotating element that floats gently away. Kram's combination of a delicate dynamic visual with a stark graphic frame creates a simultaneously jarring and sensual experience.

As the set of clicks are visualized in the colored backdrop of connected circles, the foreground displays a set of keys that represent the various clients connected to the system. In what Minar calls "God mode," he can at will press any key and take over a client with a different stream of information.

Reed Kram

www.kramdesign.com

REFLECTIONS ON EDUCATION

Reed Kram graduated from MIT in 1998. He was one of my first students at MIT and has since taught design extensively in Europe.

I am a man, 5'11" tall. I was born in Columbus, Ohio, USA. I live in an old milk factory with my woman and daughter in Stockholm. I am still baffled by Ohio. I have always traveled a great deal. In the past, I traveled for education; now I travel in my work.

My first education was technical. I knew I would never be a scientist or an engineer; however, I honestly thought I could become a twenty-first-century Renaissance man, but I knew I would never be able to teach myself. After university, I passed three years immersing myself in international culture, experimenting and doing bizarre performances. During this time I developed a style of interactive creations, and I had essentially given up on any hope of a conventional art or design education. When I showed my work to artists or designers, they could not fit it into any existing boxes, so clearly no school would take me. Luckily, I ran into John Maeda, who recognized something in my process and invited me to MIT.

When I graduated from MIT I moved to Europe. I believed that to understand the true nature of contemporary design, one had to cross cultures.

My entire education was conducted in the United States, while my experience as an educator has been solely in Europe. In the States, we are all born imperfect with imperfect families. From the time of Ralph Waldo Emerson, we have been expected to write our own destinies, and education serves to explore our possibilities. Europeans expect different results from their education. For them, it is a direct link from the past to the present—it is culture.

If I am sincere, I became an educator in part because I could not find a teacher. My interests have always been outside the boundaries of traditional disciplines, and I found there was nowhere else to go. I had reached a dead end. I felt it was my responsibility to teach.

I teach for altruistic and selfish reasons. Education gave me eyes to see the world, and I want to return the favor. But, I also teach to learn. I take courses about which I understand most of the content but not everything. The students help to fill in the blanks.

Over time, I have become a much more demanding educator—of myself and my students. There is so little time, and lately, as I push my students more, I have become more understanding of those who educated me. I was an impossible student. I was an impossible American student.

With regard to European design, any movement is considered stupid. The more educated the student, the greater the potential for the dreaded analysis paralysis: a stalled condition of logical purity and complete inaction. We must, then, draw forth so-called stupid acts. We must create a state of induced stupidity. The flow of stupidity contains the potential for greatness, and the hope for a twenty-first-century Renaissance man after all.

Gillian Crampton Smith

www.interaction-ivrea.net
EDUCATING INTERACTION DESIGNERS

Gillian Crampton Smith founded the famed Royal College of Art Computer-Related Design Unit. Since 2001, Crampton Smith has directed the Interaction Design Institute Ivrea, which aims to define the field of interaction design in this new millennium—chances are it will succeed.

When I started teaching graphic design thirty years ago (I started early!), Letraset had just been invented, but lots of printing was still done by letterpress and typeset by hand. Indeed, my introduction to graphic design was through the physical feel of setting type as a teenager. When I came to specialize in graphic design, I was teaching in a medium that had existed for five hundred years, with such Modern Movement concepts as truth to materials and the application of Gestalt psychology to graphic composition. The design of information (images, messages) was a well-understood skill that married graphic inventiveness with careful craftsmanship rooted in the material qualities (advantages and constraints) of print technology.

How different today to teach interaction design. It is not possible to teach an established craft because every three years or so the technology changes. It is no longer about designing for an audience with a shared culture and language—your audience may come from any part of the world. So, subtlety of references or plays on implicit meaning run the risk of going down like a lead balloon. Instead of absolute control over what our viewers perceive, we do not even know what size the display will be on the systems we design.

So, what are the qualities of interactive technologies, which are clearly so different from print? What is different and special about the media of computers, electronics and telecommunications?

Take film. Early film-makers drew on existing conventions: pointing the camera at a "stage," putting "chapter headings" at the start of scenes. It was not until Cecil B. DeMille and Sergei Eisenstein that a true language of film developed, one that exploited the particular qualities of the medium. Today's education must challenge young designers to discover, understand and develop the language of a new medium: interactivity.

My first ten years teaching computer-related design were spent at the Royal College of Art in London. The British art-school tradition (in which design is deeply rooted) has two main antecedents: William Morris and the Arts and Crafts movement in the nineteenth century; and the Bauhaus in the twentieth century. Morris believed in the nobility of traditional craft as an antidote to the soullessness of factory work and the banality of factory products. The Bauhaus, on the other hand, sought to unite the qualities of craft with mass-produced design. Where I now work, in Ivrea, was the home town of Adriano Olivetti. A byword for design and technological creativity, Olivetti believed in the humanization of technology, both for the factory worker and for the office worker who would use the products. Morris, the Bauhaus and Olivetti all understood that technology has a social impact. New technologies demand that we think of what to design, but also how to design it well; designing the right thing is as important as designing it right. Herein lies the second challenge for young designers: What is the right thing to design?

horatory

VISIBLE LANGUAGE WORKSHOP

E15

44

8. Beyond

There are few periods in life for lengthy reflection. In the process of closing down a major effort (the ACG) and devoting time to a new one (my new baby), I had such a period over 2003. A birth makes you ever more pensive about the life you have lived and the people who helped you to get where you are. Where is that? In my case, I am glad to say that place is still unknown. I hope to continue to meet more people in the coming years who ensure my final destination remains a healthy mystery.

Muriel Cooper was a rare visionary whom I had the fortune of meeting and sharing communication with. Most of what I know about her comes from the stories she left behind. Her sister Helene tells me of the fearlessness with which Muriel approached situations. For instance, she was famous for placing her feet on the table or desk while talking to people, whether a colleague or a complete stranger. I recently unraveled the thinking behind this trait when a researcher at the Media Lab related her interchange with Muriel on the subject. Muriel was the rare woman in the male-dominated profession of design in academia. When asked if she worried that she might make powerful businessmen feel uncomfortable, she replied, "How they feel? Think about how they make me feel all of the time."

It was Muriel who suggested I leave MIT and go to art school—the best advice I have ever received. I used to be amused by the often negative response from students when I told them they should go to art school. "So, you don't think I can cut it at MIT?" was an unfortunately common reaction. No, it was not that. I just believed that some needs might be better served elsewhere. Now, however, I feel differently. Recent events have led me to strongly believe that MIT has the potential to rise as one of the most important art schools in the world. All naysayers beware.

Housed on the fourth floor of the Media Lab's main building E15, the Visible Language Workshop (VLW) realized the world's first atelier-style approach to a learning environment for technologists. Muriel Cooper brought a wealth of book-design experience from her twenty-five-year tenure as art director of MIT Press. The charge of the VLW was to create an electronic environment to support investigation into the process of design and distribution of the then emerging digital media content.

Muriel Cooper's prophecy about the page-layout system was certainly fulfilled:

"Two phases of the graphic computer will evolve. Phase 1: Tools that emulate production tools of old media with greater speed, economy, flexibility and interaction, and Phase 2: Professional tools in the hands of non-professionals will change traditional professional practices and patterns of design and production."

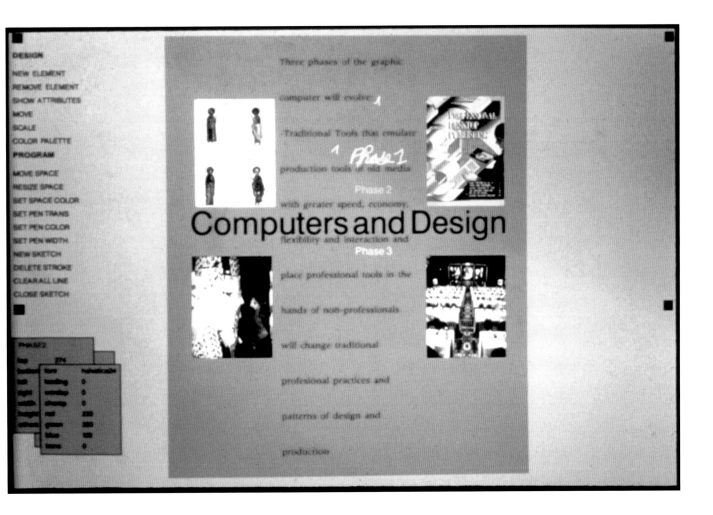

From the perspective of the computer-science world, research at the Media Lab was once viewed as "sissy." Work at the VLW fueled this derogatory viewpoint with such outlandish experiments as this early attempt at computer-aided package design.

However, when we look at the computer today and see how the process of art and design has been transformed, a cursory glance at early VLW work reveals the missing link between printed page and computer screen. There is something truly satisfying when the sissies turn out to be right.

EARLY PACKAGE-DESIGN SYSTEM
VLW, c. 1986

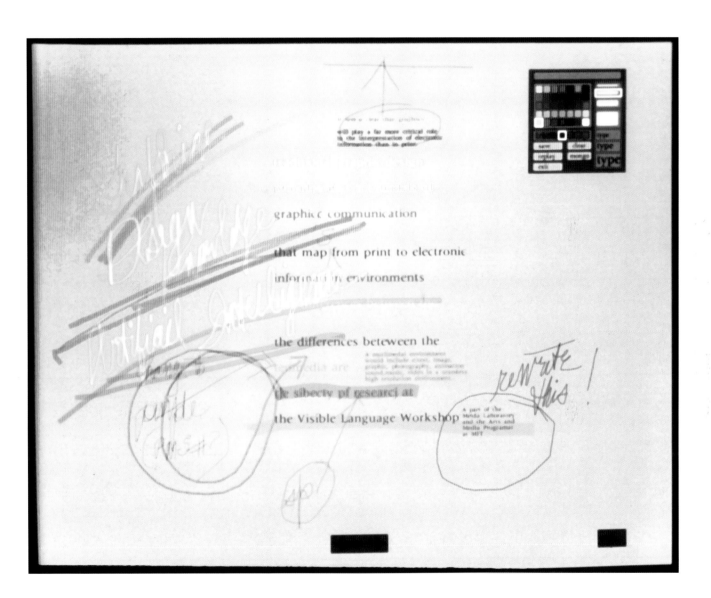

Particular attention was paid to the importance of anti-aliased fonts, so-called "fuzzy fonts." Painstaking attention to typeface selection, color, transparency, and the screen's structure placed the VLW at a visual skill level unparalleled in the computer world. The VLW's legacy continues in its graduates who blaze new ground in academia and industry worldwide. They are numerous and unstoppable, thanks to our beloved Muriel.

My first class at MIT revealed my own
ignorance of teaching, and I treasure that
memory. I strive to achieve ignorance in my
everyday life. Ignorance, of course, means that
any discovery, whether large or small, will go
unignored. That might seem contradictory, but
consider how nervous you are when you do
something for the first time because you are
unprepared. Each moment of failure feels so
much worse, and each moment of success is
so rare that when you see a positive response,
if only for a millisecond, you have the faith to
keep on moving forward.

One day I brought a computer and projector
to class. I opened up an empty Java program
skeleton, and asked the class to edit the
program as a collaborative process, whereby
one line of code was entered by each person.
This experiment revealed the students' different
styles of coding and resulted in general chaos.
A close look at the actual code shows a
clumsiness and syntactical inconsistency. The
starting applet displayed "A simple Applet," as
text on a blank white background, but by the
time we had finished the experiment, it had
changed to "A sim pull Applet" atop a decidedly
more ornate background.

```
import java.io.*;
import java.awt.*;
import java.applet.*;
import java.net.*;

public class HelloWorld extends Applet implements Runnable {

URL babble;

int globalx, globaly;
    double r;
    Thread anima;
    String s="";

    int dx, dy, s_index=0, offset;

    public void init() {

        super.init();

        //{{INIT_CONTROLS
        setLayout(null);
        resize(283,190);
        label1=new Label("A sim pull Applet", Label.CENTER);
        add(label1);
        label1.reshape(68,75,147,15);
        anima = null;

        DataInputStream d = null;
        try {
        babble = new URL(getDocumentBase(), "HelloWorld.java");
        d = new DataInputStream(babble.openStream());

        String ts;
        while((ts=d.readLine()) != null)
        {
            s = s+ts;
        }
```

A sim pull Applet

```java
        } catch (Exception e) {System.out.println("HI "+e);};
    // System.out.println(e);
    //}}
}

public boolean handleEvent(Event event) {
    return super.handleEvent(event);
}

//{{DECLARE_CONTROLS
Label label1;
//}}

public boolean mouseDown(Event e, int x, int y)
{
    double r1 = Math.random(); double r2 = Math.random();

    if (anma != null) anma.stop();
    anma = new Thread("drawing");
    anma.start();
    r = r1+r2;
    globalx = x; globaly = y;
    repaint();
    return true;
}

public boolean mouseDrag(Event e, int x, int y) {

    dx = globalx-x; dy=globaly-y;
    globalx = x; globaly = y;
    Graphics g = getGraphics();

    repaint();
    return true;
}

public void run() {
    while (true) {
        offset = (offset-2)%250;
        repaint();
        try { Thread.sleep(100); } catch (Exception e) {}
    }
}

public void paint(Graphics g) {
    int flip=0;
    Polygon poly = new Polygon();
    g.setColor(Color.white);
    Rectangle b = bounds();
    g.fillRect(0,0,b.width,b.height);
    g.setColor (Color.green);
    g.fillOval(globalx,offset+globaly,250,30  );

    g.setColor (Color.red);
    g.drawRect(0,0,size().width, size().height);
    g.setColor(Color.black);
    g.drawLine(0,0,20,20);
    g.fillOval( 20, 20, 35, 35 );
    g.setXORMode(Color.white);
    // s_index = 0;
    int i;
    for (i =0; i < 20; i++) {
        for (int j=0; j<25; j++) {
            g.drawRect(i*10, j*10, 5, 5);
            for (int k=j; k<i; k++) {
                g.drawOval(i*, (k-j)*5, (int)(r*i), (int)(r*j));
                g.setColor(new Color((i*20)%255,(j*10)%255,(k*10)%255));
                flip *= 1;
                if(flip == 1) g.drawRect(i*, (k-j)*5, i/2, j/2);
                else g.drawRect(size().width-i*j, size().height-(k-k*)*5, 2*i/3, 2*j/3);
                //g.drawString("super.int(); //{{INIT_CONTROLS setLayout(null);resize(283,190);
                            anma = null;i, j*, i, j;
            }
        }
    }
    s_index++;
    g.setColor(Color.red);
    if (s_index == s.length()) s_index = 0;
    g.drawString(""+s.charAt(s_index), globalx, globaly);
    g.setColor(Color.darkGray);
    g.drawRect(0,0,b.width-1,b.height-1);
    //System.out.println(""+s_index);
    // System.out.println(""+s.charAt(s_index));

}

}
```

As a continuation of the collaborative coding process, we attempted an experiment to better understand visual design on the computer. In the atrium of the Media Lab, we rigged up a camera on the fourth floor pointing downward; in the lower lobby, we projected the image seen from above so that the students (as pixels) could see themselves. The idea was that each student took charge and "programmed" the pixels, whether by script or direct commands.

My inspiration for this experiment was a Bauhaus story of an old Master taking his students to the gymnasium to walk on the paths of large circles to grasp the form's essence. Our experiment was difficult to set up, much less orchestrate, with an impatient bunch of understandably eager students seeking to set history in motion. The chaos that transpired was so great that I had to take a day off to recover; I learned that people are not pixels, period.

Countless variations were explored,

ranging from "slide" the pixel,

to follow the marked pixel,

to pass the pixel.

I always wonder what a session with a panel of experts at a conference achieves. Having been on many and hosted a fair share of them, I decided to put students on the spot by making them the expert speakers in an impromptu schedule of panels. This role-playing activity forced students to contribute their own perspectives. Finding that they all had fully formed opinions was the main lesson learned.

Panels: Session 2

1. Static, Physical, and Hyper-real

An object in motion stays in motion. What do computer screen do? Should it do nothing? Sho physical world? Should it go beyond? But if i recognize it anymore?

Everything has a place and context. Should als context is display screen or else virtual real

2. One shot performance vs. Continuum

When a person interacts, does he or she get only the dialogue unfold over time? Or is it understoo the person come back later? Do we need light inter interaction? What kind of contexts are there?

The singular, repeatable experience versus the forev interacting with a pool of water versus hearing a nar

3. Coding vs. Caching

Using computation, we can generate imagery. However, wha we not generate in real time? Is that an issue? Will we e to seamlessly move between drawing and computation? Can t and the same? Are they already?

What was meant was a d
The conclu

Tom White / Problem 4A

Don't drag the mouse around, it's against the rules.

(DIS)OBEYING THE RULES
Tom White, 1996

When students have a sense of humor, the learning game becomes fun. I am notorious for laying down a set of severe constraints on problem solving. White's piece wryly reminds the viewer that he is compliant, and so, hopefully, is the user of the software piece.

I often ask students to be sure to stick to black and white. The majority listens, while a small minority takes some time to understand. Rice never understood the rules and, therefore, never complied. I distinguish this behavior from the action of one who understands the rules and does not comply out of spite. The latter situation is to be avoided whenever possible.

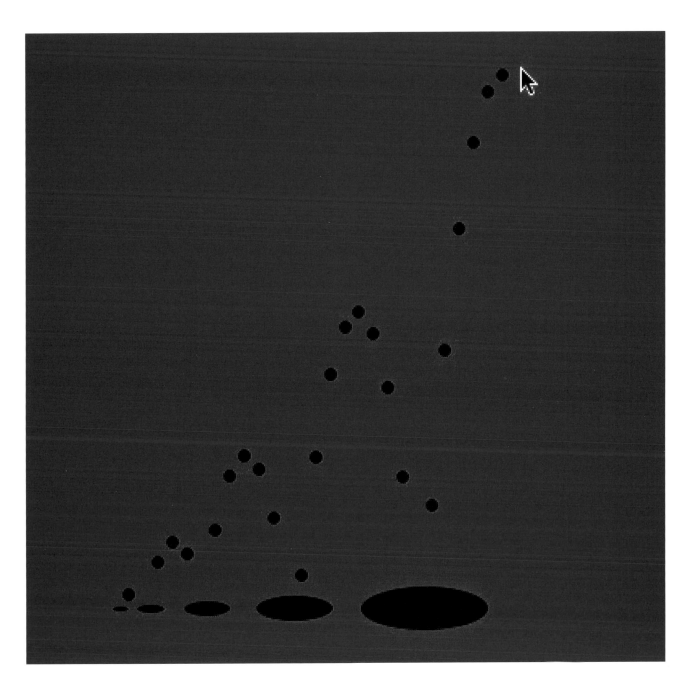

In addition to color, I often outlaw random numbers in my classes. For one assignment, I relaxed both constraints and made only a single demand: that random numbers be "handmade." Dahley cleverly uses the time measured between individual presses of the keyboard as you type to produce a set of literally handcrafted random numbers. The system builds up in the bar at the bottom of the screen as you type, and mouse clicks release the random numbers into a chromatic translation.

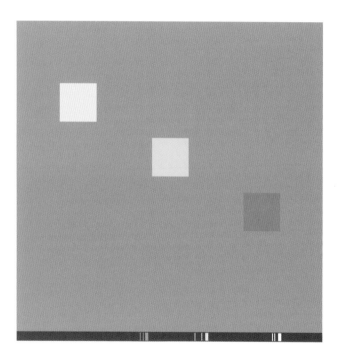

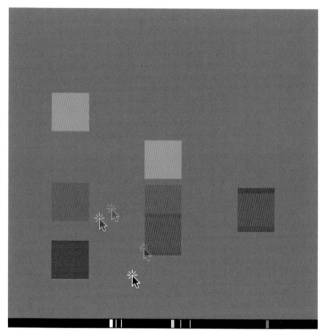

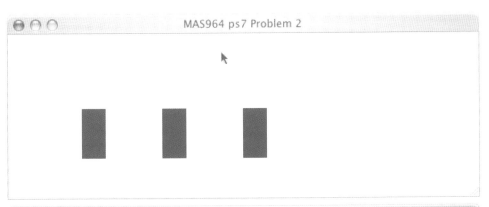

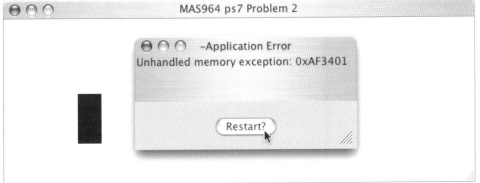

Computers perform a kind of magic on our eyes and mind. I asked for magic tricks on the screen: an object that disappeared from under the viewer's nose. Rice cleverly uses a fake error message to momentarily distract the viewer. By the time the viewer realizes the computer does not have to restart, an object has disappeared!

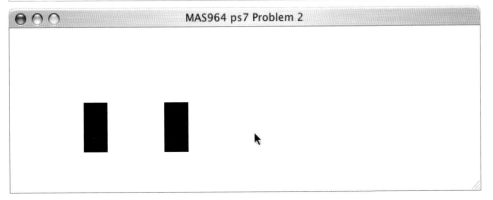

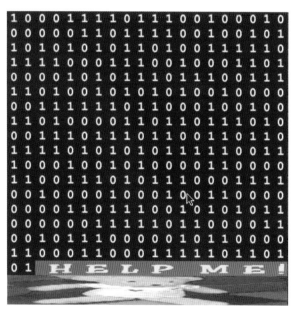

BEAR VERSION 1.0
Kelly Heaton, 1998

A prerequisite to my courses is an extremely high level of programming skill. Coming from a conventional arts background, Heaton knew nothing about coding but she never gave up. Her first computer codes bear the spirit of her fierce love of stuffed animals, which, incidentally, continues in her work today on the contemporary art scene.

A political celebrity is reinterpreted in this
accidental program, or "bug." The power of
the artistic perspective is to know how to use
a mistake to the best advantage.

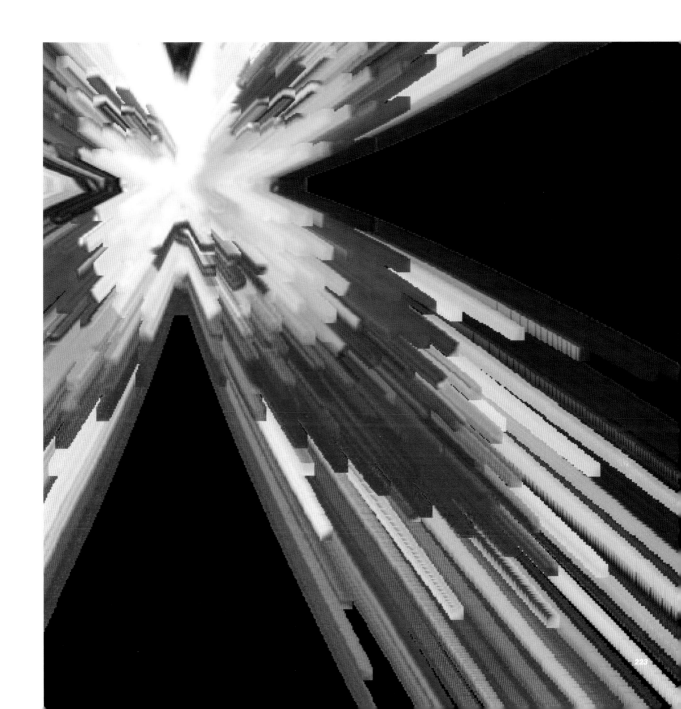

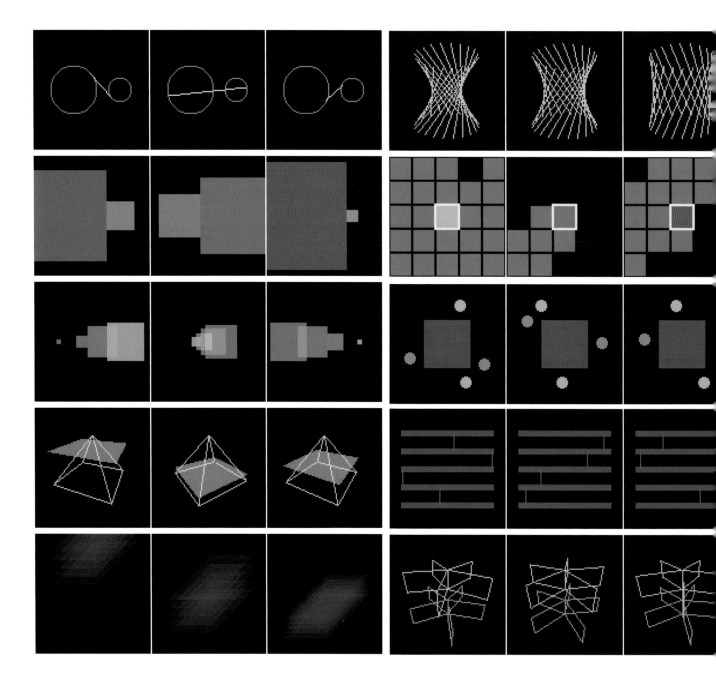

BOX OF FINE CANDIES
Casey Reas, 1999

Many people come to see me every year hoping to study with me at the Media Lab. I tell a prospective student from engineering or the sciences to get some training in design or the arts. I advise a prospective student from the arts and design to get some experience in programming or electronics. I rarely see most of these people again.

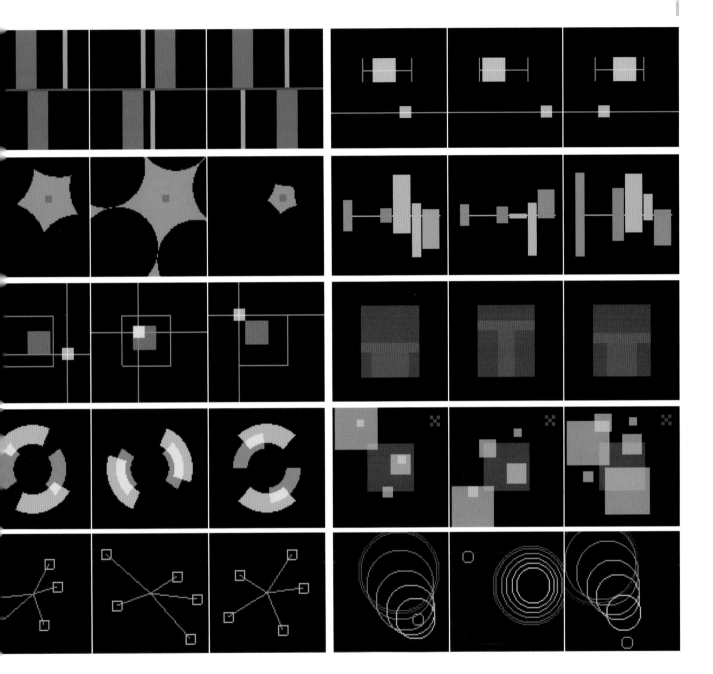

Casey Reas appeared one day, and I outlined what he needed to know. At that time, he was design director of a prominent Internet start-up, and I wrote him off as another person to vanish. A month later, he informed me that he had quit his job to study programming in earnest.

In less than a year he reappeared, laptop in hand, with a set of sixteen visual pieces that were remarkable and simply impossible. To this day, Reas surprises me and defies any notions I have of what is impossible.

Benjamin Fry

acg.media.mit.edu/people/fry
FOR I = 0

Benjamin Fry completed his Ph.D at MIT in 2004. I was introduced to Fry by Suguru Ishizaki. From the moment I met him, I knew that he would achieve far more than I could ever imagine. Watch him go.

"This is a 'for loop'," my dad said. We were sitting in front of an imperial white box reading a page of green text. It was not so much that my dad taught me programming as he planted the seed. Having shown me how to write a simple loop, he handed me an oddly colored Basic manual. And so began many years of writing software that helped feed what I later recognized as an addiction to building and making things.

Throughout my undergraduate career, I was set on user interface design as the ideal way of combining my interest in programming, and my preoccupation with graphic design, both of which had developed in parallel. Both interests began before my age was in double digits, but over the years the names of my ideal title or field evolved: at one time "programmer," later "software engineer," or from "making logos" to "advertising" to "graphic design." But, my belief that my interest lay in user interface design was undone after a year spent in industry, in the same way, I suppose, that not all mathematically and visually inclined people are made for architecture. Too little time was spent on either design or programming, and the time spent arguing about whether a design could be implemented in software was more than the time for its actual implementation. The creative part almost completely lost out in comparison to the hours spent on lengthy rationalizations and evangelizing specifications.

I returned to the MIT to join the Aesthetics and Computation Group. During my last year as an undergraduate design student, Professor Maeda had visited our class and shown a vast portfolio of software experiments. Being in a department with a passive-aggressive relationship to the computer, it was a shock for me to witness the head-on collision of what I was creating in my studio courses and what I did in the lab for my computer-science classes. It made complete sense, but I had missed the connection, not realizing that a mixture or balance existed. Until that time, I had used courses in each field to contrast the other: retreating to my computer-science courses when I wanted the comfort of a "right" answer to a problem or assignment, only to return to my graphic-design work when I began to lose hours over an unexplainable bug.

Whether I realized it or not, programming has always been a creative outlet for me, since I derive pleasure in the creation of an artifact. During my first year at the ACG, I began to shift toward using software as an expressive medium, although, at the time, I would have avoided calling it "creative" for fear of sounding presumptuous. It was not until a few years later that I received external validation that the process was "creative," when I was pleasantly surprised to be asked to show my work in an art exhibition. Software is unmistakably no less of an expressive medium or material than any I have worked in before; yet, it was only recently I began to understand how to use it in a purely creative way.

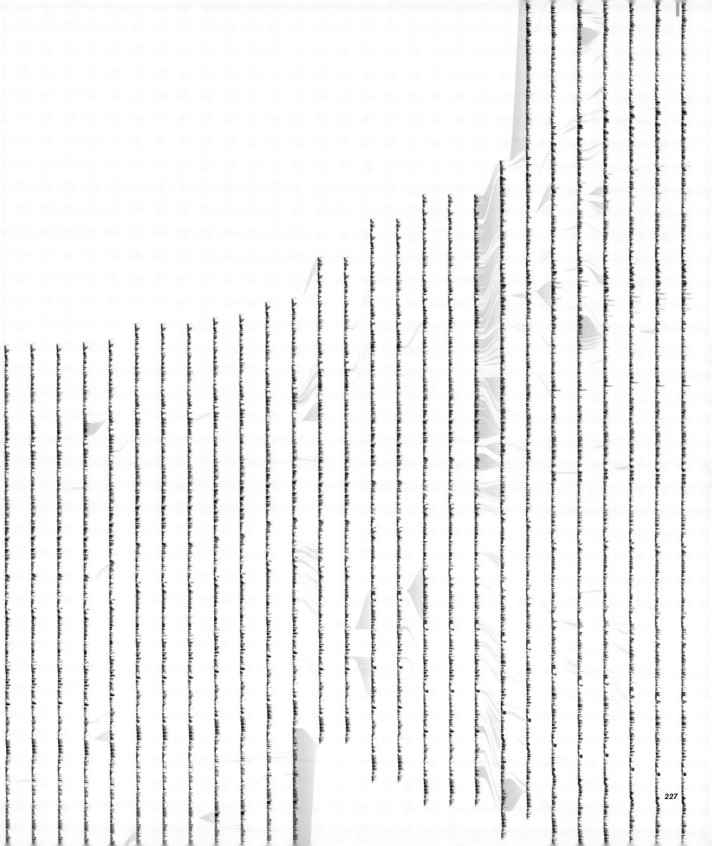

Scott Snibbe

www.snibbe.com

THE EMPTINESS OF CODE

Scott Snibbe is an artist living in San Francisco. I first met him many years ago when we were introduced by sketchmaster Bill Verplank.

At the age of ten, in 1980, I attended a computer class in which we made orange triangles glow on the screen of an Apple II by typing in a few unfamiliar words. With the incredible quality of the emitted light and the lightness of the creative process, I instantly knew what I wanted to do with my life. However, it was difficult for me to understand exactly where to locate the artwork in this medium. My mind was filled with questions: How does language create images? How do images remain when the language that creates them disappears from the computer's memory? Where do code and images go when I turn off the computer? Where are they while the computer is running?

In college, computer science answered these questions with a linear model: Computation begins outside the processor in the programmer's algorithmic thinking and in the program text that embodies these thoughts. Compilers distill the program text into machine instructions, and the processor interprets these instructions to move numbers within memory or to mathematically recombine them. Finally, outputs are "side effects" that happen when the ones and zeros in memory are electronically converted to variations in light on monitors.

According to this computer model, the program text is the cause of the image. However, the program text itself seems interdependent on all other aspects of computation. Indeed, to see the program text on the screen, another program must convert the numeric representation of the text into modulated light. A print-out of the program text likewise results after another program has interpreted the characters of the text as letters, and then generated printed characters as an output side effect. Even a program that is handwritten on a piece of paper relies on the model of the computer held in the programmer's mind. Any representation of the program's text seems entirely interdependent on the computer model; so, calling the program text the cause of the output is inaccurate. This interconnectedness of process, image and the viewer's mind reminds me of the Buddhist question, "Why is it that we see the letter 'M' on a page, instead of a small squiggle of ink?"

This question appears in the Buddhist teaching on Emptiness, which asserts that all things exist interdependently with all other things, both materially and conceptually. Every material part of our body originates from somewhere else; and our thoughts, language, and personalities emerge entirely from interactions with others. It is our consciousness that creates artificial categories from the interdependent continuum of existence. Within this framework, computation is understood as an interdependent chain of cause and effect, with no original or primary cause. No part of the continuum from programmer to program, processor to display, and display to viewer can be removed without breaking the computational chain.

This view contradicts the idea that the image or animation produced by a computational artwork is the entire work of art. It also denies, albeit more subtly, that the program text is the creative locus in computational art; a piece of code is not alive in the way a computational system is. Code is not only invisible in an executing system, it is also unextractable, having been incorporated into unreadable machine instructions. Computational artwork exists only as a continuation of the programmer's thoughts through the computational medium and into the mind of the viewer. There is no way to remove or separate these components.

The year is 2004, and I am restless. There is a great deal of work to do, and yet the economic bust of the dot.com era has stunted innovation and its related fearlessness. The usual bastions of youthful anarchy—art schools—are at a standstill due to the disruptive force of technology. "What is it?" "Which department should own it?" "Do we really need it?" "It's nothing more than a tool, so why make such a big deal?" I am constantly surprised by how little progress is being made to embrace digital media in new ways; instead, it is juggled like a hot potato around art and design departments.

Meantime, I have gathered a small team of extremely talented creatives to turn the clock back on the digital revolution to 1984. The Aesthetics and Computation Group is now the Physical Language Workshop (PLW). The reason why it is "physical" and not "visual" will become evident over time. At the time of the ACG's conception, many people found odd the juxtaposition of the two words "aesthetics" and "computation," whereas today it seems quite common and positive. I have heard one interpretation of "physical language" as something offensive, like a rude physical gesture. I would like to think it incorporates all the bad, all the good, and more.

The PLW is rewinding the version number on commonly used software from 10, 9, and 8 to 1.0 to rethink our creative role in respect to the computer. By returning to the origins of creativity on the computer, we hope to factor in the web and e-commerce from the ground up, hopefully encouraging the digital arts to flourish in new and meaningful ways. We call this movement in creativity and technology "OpenAtelier."

OpenAtelier is an open-source infrastructure for creative activity on the web. The web browser becomes the primary vehicle for editing, annotating, and sharing digital media from any point in the world. Since most computers do not ship with working software, OpenAtelier will be able to serve as an immediately accessible gateway to a modern digital hub. This hub we believe will mark a new age of digital creative commerce for everyone.

OpenAtelier

The PLW now has a working prototype for a
network-based drawing system that saves files
to the web. The dialog box for handling files is a
thin visual skin over a database query that can
be flexibly defined. By placing data centrally on
the web, many people can edit it—a commonly
accepted contemporary high-tech scenario—the
twist, here, is that the tools, in addition to the
data, reside on the web.

Mariana Baca, Carlos Rocha, Jessica Rosenkrantz, Marc Schwartz, 2003

A variety of prototype applications for editing
such things as photos and sound currently live
on the web. Here, an experimental system for
easily creating new tools and extensions (or
plug-ins) to existing tools has been produced.
The aim is to build a new marketplace around
these types of systems developed within
OpenAtelier.

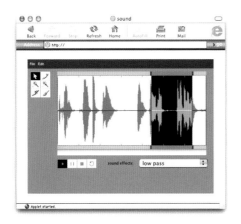

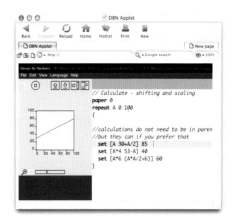

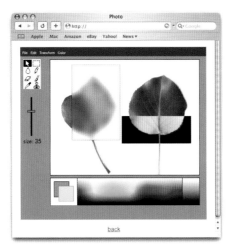

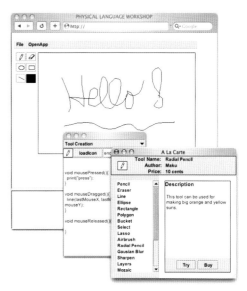

Video editing is data intensive, a fact that is increasingly accommodated on modern computers. However, up until now editing videos over the web has been hindered. Seo has developed a prototype application whereby a thin client is wrapped over a powerful back-end server that delivers on demand thumbnails and clips. The web application remains small and the server does the bulk of the work.

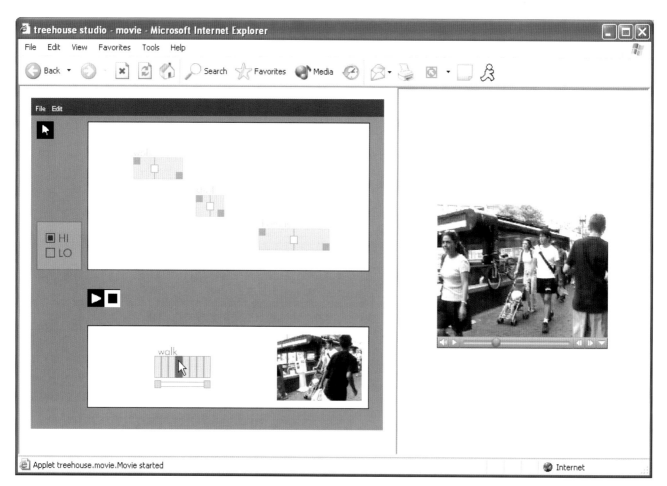

ONLINE CAFE SYSTEM

Mimi Liu, Ricarose Roque, 2003

New services are being developed to share and
perhaps even sell visual goods created using
online tools. A virtual café is being constructed
in which visual drawings become virtual food in
a conversation-themed environment.

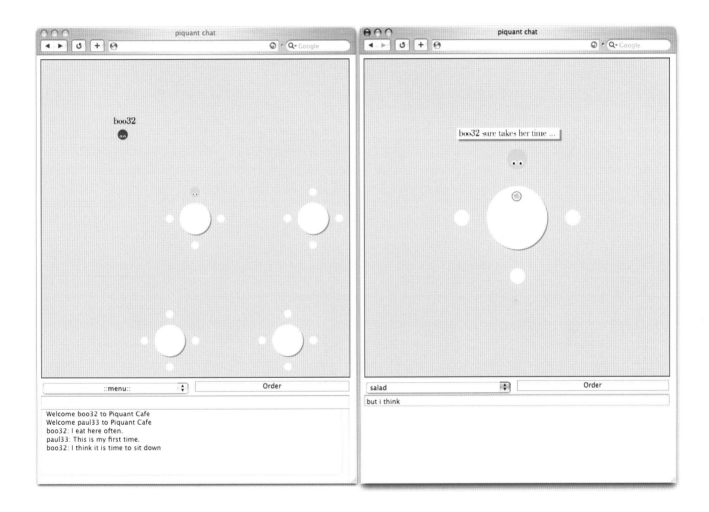

DISPLAY ARRAY AND ONLINE GALLERY SYSTEM
Allen Rabinovich, Patrick Menard, 2003

Many online tools will soon be able to fuel a variety of scenarios that are not purely virtual. From a gallery-building system by Rabinovich to Menard's array of iMacs that is a generic reconfigurable display device for any content within the OpenAtelier world, digital living will become just as physical as it is virtual.

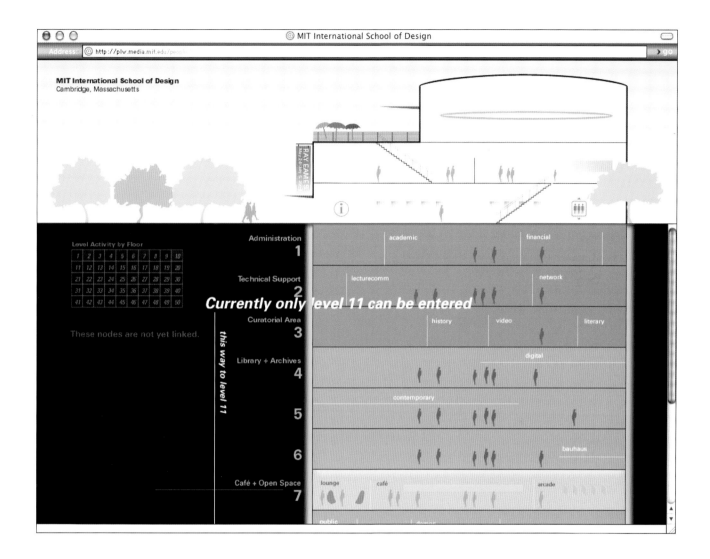

Address: http://plw.media.mit.edu/peo

MIT International School of Design
Cambridge, Massachusetts

Level Activity by Floor

1	2	3	4	5	6	7	8	9	10
11	12	13	14	15	16	17	18	19	20
21	22	23	24	25	26	27	28	29	30
31	32	33	34	35	36	37	38	39	40
41	42	43	44	45	46	47	48	49	50

These nodes are not yet linked.

this way to level 11

Currently only level 11 can be entered

Administration **1** — academic — financial

Technical Support **2** — lecturecomm — network

Curatorial Area **3** — history — video — literary

Library + Archives **4** — digital

5 — contemporary

6 — bauhaus

Café + Open Space **7** — lounge — café — arcade

public

ONLINE DIGITAL BAUHAUS
John Maeda with many future collaborators, 2010

The ultimate goal of the PLW is to use all of its momentum to realize a Bauhaus of the twenty-first century that exists completely online. We are working on a variety of scenarios to make this happen, and OpenAtelier is only the first step towards the ultimate goal. See you there!

Acknowledgments

I would not have been able to create this book were it not for the many students with whom I have had the fortune of working over the last eight years: in the Aesthetics and Computation Group (listed chronologically): Sawad Brooks, Chloe Chao, Matthew Grenby, Bill Keays, David Small, Douglas Soo, Tom White, Peter Cho, Rich DeVaul, Elise Co, Benjamin Fry, Axel Kilian, Golan Levin, Casey Reas, Jared Schiffman, Max Van Kleek, Joshua Nimoy, Nikita Pashenkov, Megan Galbraith, Simon Greenwold, Justin Manor; in my classes at MIT (listed chronologically): Joey Berzowska, Andrew Dahley, Matthew Gorbet, Nelson Minar, Peter Rice, Nitin Sawney, Phillip Tiongson, Manish Tuteja, Wandy Sae-Tan, Ingeborg Endter, Bradley Geilfuss, Maria Redin, Tara Rosenberger, Scott Snibbe, Bill Verplank, Fernanda Viegas, Marc Downie, Elizabeth Haley, Kelly Heaton, Yuri Ivanov, Matthew Lau, Sunil Vemuri, Ben Balas, Bruce Chang, Lauren Dubick, Catherine Foo, Christopher McGillicuddy, Nick DeMarco, Casey Muller, Tuyet Nguyen, Jumaane Jeffries, Jocelyn Lin, Philip Tan, Hoeteck Wee, Cameron Marlon, Dana Spiegel, Hannes Vilhjalmsson, Carson Reynolds, Shyam Krishnamoorthy, Megumi Ando, Oskar Bruening, Joy Forsythe, Ben Gallup, Anna Lee, Andy Leiserson, Annie Lie, Ben Maron, Alex Mekelburg, Keinosuke Miyanaga, Neha Bhooshan, Tony Ferreira, Terry Gaige, Bob Hall, Daniel McAnulty, Max Planck, Allen Rabinovich, Afsheen Rais-Rohani, Shuehan Liang, Vishy Venugoplan, Margarita Dekoli, Kelly Dobson, Jeana Frost, Tim Hirzel, Noah Luken, Gian Pangaro, James Patten, Michael Rosenblatt, Parul Vora, Stephanie Dahlquist, Nadya Direkova, Ercument Gorgul, Limor Fried, Sophia Han, Sonya Huang, Alex Johnson, Gregory Jones, Zahra Kanji, Devang Kothari, Adam Kraft, Yanni Loukissas, Christine Liu, Mimi Lui, Seth Mastin, Patrick Menard, Jason Mueller, Sandy Pae, Dan Sura, Cesar Villareal, William Williams, Alex Wong, Xi Zhang, Mariana Baca, Annie Ding, Elaine Lai, Quinn Mahoney, David Mellis, Ricarose Roque, Jessica Rosenkrantz, Amanda Smith, Alice Suh, Ran Tao, Aileen Wu. If I have missed listing a student here, the mistake was not intentional, and I am sorry.

The faculty of the Media Lab has provided an unparalleled support group for any avant-garde activity or otherwise wacky set of ideas: Dan Ariely, Walter Bender, Stephen Benton, Bruce Blumberg, V. Michael Bove, Jr., Cynthia Breazeal, David Cavallo, Ike Chuang, Chris Csikszentmihályi, Glorianna Davenport, Judith Donath, Neil Gershenfeld, Hiroshi Ishii, Joe Jacobson, Kent Larson, Henry Lieberman, Andrew Lippman, Tod Machover, Pattie Maes, Scott Manalis, Bakhtiar Mikhak, Marvin Minsky, William J. Mitchell, Nicholas Negroponte, Seymour Papert, Joe Paradiso, Sandy Pentland, Roz Picard, David P. Reed, Mitchel Resnick, Deb Roy, Christopher Schmandt, Ted Selker, Barry Vercoe. The infrastructure of the Media Lab has been kept safe and robustly operating by Stephen Berezansky, Michail Bletsas, Jon Ferguson, Jeannie Finks, Will Glesnes, Tom Greene, Elizabeth Harvey-Forsythe, Jane Wojcik, Chi Yuen. The internal machinery of the Lab works fine not due to the machines but thanks to the people, especially the incredible administration team: Ramona Allen, Susan Bottari, Betsy Chimento, Valerie Chin, Deborah Cohen, Missy Corley, Kevin Davis, John DiFrancesco, Julie Fresina, Polly Guggenheim, Ellen Hoffman, Robens Joseph, Alexandra Kahn, Jacqueline Karaaslanian, Margaret Kelly-Savic, Teresa Kratman, Sherry Lassiter, Nia Lewis, Betty Lou McClanahan, Keith Odom, Linda Peterson, Peter Rombult, Stacie Slotnick, Brian Spires, Carolyn Stoeber, Matthew Tragert, Greg Tucker, Stephen Whitney, Deborah Widener, John Archambault, Charleen Benjamin, Lisa Breede, Heather Childress, Maureen Coleman, Tracy Daniels, Sarah Dionne, Liz Farley, Liz Hennessey, Michael Houlihan, Aileen Kawabe, Cornelle King, Lynne Lenker, Lisa Lieberson, Tatyana Lugovskaya, David Martin, Michelle Merck, Patricia Solakoff, Ysis Soto, Kristie Thompson, Virginia Todman, Pei Wang.

I owe a sincere thanks to the administration support I have personally received from Connie Van Rheenen, Elizabeth Marzloff, Heather Childress, and Felice Gardner. Without their daily help, I would not be able to help anyone.

The whole idea of going into education was sparked by a variety of people whom I have thanked in *MAEDA@MEDIA*. Of those, I must thank most Michio Iwaki for suggesting that I create a battalion of talents that would put me out of business ... or, at least, I think I owe Mr Iwaki thanks in this area (smile). In addition, the famed designer Mitsuo Katsui was instrumental in shaping my vision for the future as both an educator and a practitioner. Mr. Katsui has always filled me with the hope that you can do both while leading an honest, simple life.

I must give special thanks to the contributors to this book: Casey Reas, John Simon, Jr., David Small, Martin Wattenberg, Peter Cho, Yugo Nakamura, Golan Levin, Joshua Davis, Elise Co, Daniel Rozin, Reed Kram, Gillian Crampton Smith, Benjamin Fry, and Scott Snibbe. Their combined contributions have added an important extra dimension to this book that I thought would be indispensable. Looking at the final product, I know I was right.

I had a fantasy of producing this book with a design assistant. I would like to thank Anne Baumgardner for heeding my call, and also for being understanding when we learned that I do not know how to have a design assistant help me. In the end, I did the book myself, again. Somehow my hands still work, and I am grateful to the RSI God for keeping them intact.

Lucas Dietrich and Catherine Hall edited this book into shape, and I owe them my thanks!

Finally, and most importantly, to my family: my wife Kris and children Mika, Rie, Saaya, and Naoko. I hope that I will eventually be able to better balance health, family, and work.

Index

John Maeda

Muriel Cooper professor of media arts and sciences at the Media Laboratory of the Massachusetts Institute of Technology.

Amidst all the attention given to the sciences as to how they can lead to the cure of all diseases and daily problems of mankind, I believe that the biggest breakthrough will be the realization that the arts, which are conventionally considered "useless," will be recognized as the whole reason why we ever try to live longer or live more prosperously. The arts are the science of enjoying life. *The New York Times,* 11 November 2003